THE BEST DEVOTIONS OF

Patsy Clairmont

WOMEN OF FAITH™

THE BEST DEVOTIONS OF

Patsy Clairmont

ZONDERVAN™

GRAND RAPIDS, MICHIGAN 49530

ZONDERVAN™

The Best Devotions of Patsy Clairmont
Copyright © 2001 by Patsy Clairmont

Requests for information should be addressed to:
Zondervan, *Grand Rapids, Michigan 49530*

Library of Congress Cataloging-in-Publication Data

Clairmont, Patsy.
     The best devotions of Patsy Clairmont/Patsy Clairmont.
        p. cm.
     ISBN 0-310-24174-X
     1. Christian women—Prayer-books and devotions—English.
    I. Title.
    BV4844 .C55 2001
    242'.643—dc21
                                     2001026807

Published in association with the literary agency of Alive Communications, Inc., 7680 Goddard Street, Suite 200, Colorado Springs, CO 80920.

Interior design by Beth Shagene

Printed in the United States of America

---

01 02 03 04 05 06 07 08 /❖ DC/ 10 9 8 7 6 5 4 3 2 1

Patti, welcome to the family
May the years ahead be the best yet

Contents

Foreword by Barbara Johnson

As amazing as it may seem to those who know us well, folks occasionally get me mixed up with Patsy Clairmont. It's amazing because we're actually so different. For example, Patsy is short and tiny, and I am, well, *not* short and *not* tiny! Perhaps people confuse us because we both love to laugh, and we write about the things that tickle us. After Patsy wrote a book titled *God Uses Cracked Pots* and I wrote *Stick a Geranium in Your Hat and Be Happy,* one woman came up to my book table somewhere and said, "I want that book called *Stick a Geranium in Your Cracked Pot*"! Well, *that* made us laugh, for sure!

Let me tell you what it's like to have a friend like Patsy. Better yet, let me show you. Pour yourself a cup of tea (peppermint is Patsy's favorite), settle into your favorite chair, kick off your shoes, then curl up with this collection of Patsy's most popular essays and devotionals and find yourself immediately drawn into her circle of friends. Patsy stands just five-feet-nothing, but she has a long, tall gift when it comes to telling and teaching. She writes about what's both real and ridiculous with delightfully turned phrases and dead-on descriptions that make us all wish we had her colorful command of giggle-graced language. She's a fabulous storyteller, and she writes her tales of lessons learned and laughter shared exactly as she tells them in person — with unleashed silliness and heartfelt truth. In her witty way she exactly describes not only how her own emotions get tangled into rambunctious knots of hormones when she's confronted by problems and predicaments but also how most of us respond to those situations too. For example, in her essay titled "Calming Faith," she perfectly sums up my own ambivalent feelings about those unruffled folks who never seem to get flustered or harried. "I've always admired laid-back people," she says, "when I wasn't aggravated by their seeming lack of gumption."

And she certainly has my driving habits down to a tee when she describes her own. For example, in "The Best-Laid Plans" she says, "I'm not a back-up kind of woman, I'm more of your full-speed-ahead kind of gal." What a coincidence: That's my favorite speed and direction too!

Patsy is a head-over-heels grandmother to grandson Justine, a devoted mom to sons Marty and Jason and their wives Danya and Patti, and a loving and supportive wife to Les, her husband of thirty-nine years. She is an artist with words and also with the elements of color and style. Being one who has a hard time deciding which doormat to choose at K-Mart, I marvel at the way Patsy can decorate an entire home right down to the tiniest detail, choosing colors and patterns I would never have dreamed of combining and somehow creating a setting that could inspire a whole year of *House Beautiful.* (Of course, she's had a little more experience at home-decorating than I have. Patsy and Les have moved *thirty-two times!)*

To see Patsy's zany moments on stage and to read her fun-filled observations on life, you'd never guess the difficult background that launched her into this ministry that brings joy and insight to thousands. But it's true. Patsy has been on a first-name basis with fear and disappointment. She dropped out of high school, married young, became a two-pack-a-day smoker, and soon found herself trapped in her home by a crippling emotional condition now known as agoraphobia. She's watched her sweet mother slowly fade into a haze of dementia, and she had her life change in an instant when Les suffered a fall that left him permanently disabled. Yet there she is today, a diminutive (non-smoking) dynamo of wit and wisdom expounding on life's foibles and God's gracious goodness to thousands of listeners and readers. She has thrilled audiences in every major city in the nation— even at a gathering of military officials at the Pentagon in Washington, D.C.!

Patsy eagerly shares her humble status as someone God rescued from the pit, and she's quick to throw the Lord's lifeline of love to those who today feel lost in pits of their own. Her lighthearted approach combined with a vast knowledge of Scripture makes her a living, breathing Sunday school lesson. As someone wisely observed, spend time with Patsy Clairmont, and "you find yourself laughing God's truths right into your heart."

Help . . . Now!

O LORD, come quickly to help me.
PSALM 70:1

Do you ever just want to throw back your head and bellow, "Gimme a break"? Life has a way of mounting up until we are slumping down. Soon our joyful noises turn into grumpy groans.

Well, we are not alone. For I hear whimperings of men, women, the rich, the poor, the young, and the old echo throughout the pages of Scripture. You may not find them using the phrase, "Gimme a break," but some of their verbiage vibrates with attitude. That attitude proclaims, "I've had enough, I've gone far enough, I've given way too much, and I'm not doing this anymore."

I noticed the Israelites wanted a break from their monotonous manna menu.

Sautéed or flambéed, the historical Tony-the-Tiger-like flakes were making the weary wayfarers hysterical. Day in, day out, the manna fell from heaven, and Mom served the same old sweet-tasting food. Why, the Israelites finally became so disgruntled they even wanted to backtrack to Egypt to chow down on smelly leeks and stinky onions. I guess they thought halitosis was better than one more helping of Mama's manna.

Then there was Sarah, wife of Abraham. Soon she was fed up with her servant girl Hagar and Hagar's son,

Ishmael. This was the second blowup between Sarah and the hired help; only this time Sarah wanted a permanent break from the pair. (Ever felt that way about someone?) She wanted Hagar and Ishmael out of her face, her family, and her fortune. So Abraham complied with Sarah's wishes and sent the pair packing with only the barest of essentials: bread and water.

Speaking of water, I wonder during Noah's boat-building days if his wife ever needed a break from his constant ark involvement? Scripture doesn't tell us her reaction to those years, but I can imagine, if she was anything like us, that she too must have thought, "C'mon, enough is enough! Gimme a break." The desire for an intermission must have multiplied when they were actually bobbing atop mountain peaks with their rowdy cargo.

I watch young moms board airplanes (arks) toting babies and all the endless, yet necessary, paraphernalia (cargo), and I wonder how they do it. I do catch glimpses of their frayed nerves and exhaustion, and I sometimes see in their eyes neon signs that flash, "Gimme a break ... please!"

I'm not sure David said "please," but I do hear him plead frequently in the Psalms for a reprieve from his enemies. Check out Psalm 70:1, 5: "Hasten, O God, to save me; O Lord, come quickly to help me. . . . You are my help and my deliverer; O Lord, do not delay."

David needed a break *now*. He was pleading with the Lord of the universe to drop everything else he was doing and rescue him. *Now* is usually when I need my help as well. That's because I tend to let things—activities, demands, mail, dishes, bills, laundry, telephone messages, people's expectations—pile up until I'm howling for help and blubbering the blues.

Jonah was a fellow who sure understood blubbering. In fact, he was taking a sea sabbatical when he found himself encased in blubber. Jonah took a self-appointed break, and it almost broke him. Once on land again it wasn't long before he was back in blubber; this time it was his own, as he wailed and whined that life and people were so difficult he wanted a permanent break. As a matter of fact, he just wanted to die.

It's obvious that, as long as we can find a reflection in the mirror, we will long for a break. And that's not wrong. Many times it's imperative if we're to avoid breaking. But other times, when we reach the end of our strength, wisdom, and personal resources, we enter into the beginning of his glorious provisions. And that's a wondrous place to be.

Dear Lord, like a child with her mom, when I say now, I mean right now! Thank you for not always dropping everything in the universe and rushing to my rescue. Instead, you have allowed me to feel my neediness and experience my limitations so I will understand that it is you who will (eventually) save me. I don't want to refuse your perfect plan; I want to find refuge in you. Then I will have the stamina to make it to the end. Amen.

The Best-Laid Plans

The LORD is near to all who call on him.
PSALM 145:18

I'm afraid my husband took this thought, "Gimme a break," a little too literally. Last week he fell in our kitchen and suffered a triple fracture to his ankle. Now he is in a cast, on crutches, and is definitely taking a break as well as having one. Whereas I, who thought I was going to take a break from a busy year of travel and speaking, find myself galloping around our premises caring for my beloved . . . hand and, yep, foot.

Now don't get me wrong; I'm grateful to be Les's nurse. I wouldn't want to be anywhere but with him. It's just that life takes so many unexpected twists and turns right in the middle of some of our best-laid plans. We had moved two weeks before Les's fall, and we both had high expectations of how we would settle into our new abode. Now our teamwork has turned into me-work. To tell you the truth, I'm not that handy.

I think the first sign that we were in for some interesting days, with Les laid up and me at the helm, was minutes after his fall. Our friend Dan was coming to assist our son Marty in maneuvering my injured husband to the car. Marty suggested I turn on the porch light for Dan's arrival. I dashed to the front door, and instead of turning on the light, I rang the doorbell. No, I can't tell you why I did that. Panicked? Possibly. Menopausal? Definitely. Space cadet? Precisely.

Since Les broke his right ankle, I have become the designated driver. Oh, boy, Les has been waiting for this chance — payback time for years of my advising him how to drive. Before I even got out of our yard for our first visit to the doctor, I came under Les's tutelage. Our new home has a rather long driveway that I have to back out of, and I'm not a back-up kind of woman. I'm more your full-speed-ahead kind of gal. My car's backseat window ledge is designed too high for me to see to back up, so I have to rely on my side mirrors. For some reason I can't stay on a straight-mirrored course, and we looked like a Weeble. (You know, those round-bottomed toys children have that wobble all over.) I was in the flower beds, then off the other side brushing the tree trunks, and then back over to the grass and onto the sidewalk before finally reaching the road. Les was amazed. Well, amazed might be under-stating his response. I watched as concern spread across his face (like hives). He seemed to realize he had several months of these yard exits to live through — and so does the yard.

Not only am I not great at backing up, but I'm also not that impressive at climbing up. Yet up is where I needed to go to pound the nails in the brackets to hold the cur-tains in the living room. Les looked pale as he observed me ascending the ladder. I assured him I could handle this task. But when I attempted to pound the itsy-bitsy nail into the wood, I dropped the bracket. I scampered down, scaled back up, and promptly dropped the ham-mer. Down the ladder I scurried again, grabbed the ham-mer, and made my way back up to the ceiling . . . huffing and puffing. (This was more aerobic than a StairMaster.) After the third drop (this time it was the nail), Les's head also dropped as he slowly shook it back and forth. Okay, okay, Bob Vila I'm not.

Although I did try a Vila-approach in our bathroom. I wanted to hang a cupboard that was heavy, and Les said I would have to nail it into the studs. One night I began to thump on the wall trying to detect the sound difference between wallboard and wood (as if I would know). Les heard my Morse code taps and jogged in on his crutches to prevent me from inadvertently ripping out a wall with my cupboard. O ye of little faith.

Les then sent me to the store to buy a stud finder so we could "do it right." I made my way to the hardware department but couldn't locate the stud finders. Two men were working in that department, but I was hesitant to ask them because I was concerned they would think I was being fresh. Finally I blurted out, "Where are your stud finders?" They smiled. They knew where they were, but they couldn't figure out how they worked or what size batteries they needed. (That made me feel a lot better.)

Then I had them direct me to the toggle screws. I needed one, only one, to mount the toilet-paper holder. Uncertain which of the three thousand screws was correct, I purchased thirty-five of them to improve my odds of "doing it right." Yep, you guessed it: they were all wrong.

C'mon, folks, gimme a break. I'm the one with a loose screw if I think I can do all these unnatural tasks. (Although I now know how to identify a stud finder and what kind of batteries it takes. I can even operate the thing.) I'm doing better backing the car out of the driveway, and with the exception of our glider, a tree, and several flowers, I've hardly rammed into anything. I've also learned when I need to put up curtain brackets to call Bob Vila. And when I need a break, even in the midst of twists and turns, to call upon the Lord.

Thank you, Lord Jesus, for hearing my cry and for walking me through my slips and falls. Amen.

Calming Faith

He maketh me to lie down in green pastures:
he leadeth me beside the still waters.

PSALM 23:2 KJV

The sweet psalmist David sang of calming faith. Lean in and listen to a line of this beloved recital: "He maketh me to lie down in green pastures: he leadeth me beside the still waters."

Notice David sang of how the Lord "maketh" and the Lord "leadeth." In other words, young David didn't come up with the idea to stop and rest in the lush pastureland. His youthful vitality probably vied for higher ground. David was probably humming bee-bop, and the Lord was saying, "Stop." The Lord knew that the shepherd boy and the sheep needed a break.

David then points out that he had to be led by the Lord to the still waters. I wonder if David had to be led because he was naturally drawn to the excitement of the rushing waters? It certainly is that way with us. Left to our own agendas, we either run at breakneck speeds right past the pasture, enamored with our frenzied pace, or sit in parched misery. The Shepherd, who understands our naiveté and our humanity (not to mention our sheeplike stupidity), intervenes on our behalf to guide us with a strong hand onto a quiet path and into a calmer faith.

Yep, a calmer faith. That's the quiet place within us where we don't get whiplash every time life tosses us a curve. Where we don't revolt when his plan and ours conflict. Where we relax (versus stew, sweat, and swear) in the midst of an answerless season. Where we accept (and expect) deserts in our spiritual journey as surely as we do joy. Where we are not intimidated or persuaded by other people's agendas but moved only by him. Where we weep in repentance, sleep in peace, live in fullness, and sing of victory.

Ultimately our life in Christ makes us winners. And being winners in the Lord means that nothing we go through is for naught. There is just something about knowing that my failures, others' failures, hardships, mistakes, losses, and pain have meaning. For me, that understanding eases some of the agony of life and encourages me to keep on keeping on.

If you asked those who know me well, they would tell you I am a reactive woman. Often overstated in my responses, I have knots on my cranium from bouncing off ceilings. I've always admired laid-back people (when I wasn't aggravated by their seeming lack of gumption). I know I need to settle down, but I'm wired tightly. Even though some of those wires seem frayed (like the ones that connect my thoughts), I can't nestle down in the green pastures long enough to enjoy the feast of his provision. It's also difficult for me to stay at the water's edge to quench my thirst, because I'm busy splashing around in the shallowness of my own agenda. Imagine giving up Niagara Falls for a dripping faucet.

I'm grateful the Lord maketh and the Lord leadeth, for I needeth in a big way! I needeth the One who madeth me to holdeth me together. When I am irrational, irksome, or irate, I need the Shepherd of this willful sheep to maketh me still and sane. That way, instead of telling off tellers, I can extend courtesy. Instead of setting my husband straight, I can extend understanding. Instead of having all the answers, I can extend a listening ear.

Perhaps that is why the Lord brought David to the pasture and the water's edge. He knew this young boy would one day be an influential king, and he would need to know how to be still, understanding, attentive, courteous, and calm. The Lord knew David would have to deal with critical issues both politically and personally. He knew the king would need to know where to go when life became too much, when he needed to be restored in his soul, when he just plain needed a break.

When you need a break, where do you tend to go? The mountains? A valley? A pastureland? The water's edge?

Wherever each of us chooses, we all know what it feels like to be at rest. And we all long for that more sane lifestyle rather than being overwhelmed. But are we willing to leave the press long enough to lie down in the soothing green pastures and to be led by the still waters of his provision? That, my friend, is not resort living but restored living. And each of us needs it.

☼

Thank you, Lord, for your strong hand lest I miss the resting places and the water's edge. For there you help me to understand some of life's mystery, and you restore my languid soul. I ask you to still my frantic heart and calm my shaky faith in Jesus' name. Amen.

Songs of the Heart

The Lord GOD is my strength, and He has made my feet like
hinds' feet, and makes me walk on my high places.
HABAKKUK 3:19 NASB

Have you noticed that we tend to be thematic people? And that other people's themes are easier to identify than our own? Throughout the years, I've had several consistent life themes that have slid in and out of my repertoire.

When I was an agoraphobic, my theme song sounded more like a dirge. "I can't," "It's too difficult," and "I'm afraid" were just a few of the phrases in my discordant refrain. Every day and every task seemed overwhelming. I gave up on a lot of life and gave in to fear as my scary companion. People tried to help me find a more melodic song to sing, but my mournful minuet with fear continued like a long-playing record.

In time people's tolerance waned. Avoiding me became easier than listening to my nerve-wracking recital. I guess they just needed a break. Eventually, even I tired of hearing my own broken-record whine.

That sad season in my life reminds me of a record my older brother Don used to enjoy when we were young: "The Little White Cloud that Cried" by Johnnie Ray. Don played it repeatedly day after day, week after week.

C'mon, folks, how many times can one listen to a crying cumulus? I'm sure that's how people felt about me.

Gradually I moved into a different tempo, one that was more upbeat. I noticed that people didn't make such wide circles to skirt around me. Some were even drawn into my circle by the new song they were hearing. I guess "Singin' in the Rain" was easier to listen to than my former melancholy rendition of "Stormy Weather."

Ruth the Moabitess didn't sing in the rain, but she must have sung amidst the grain for her delightful spirit was immediately noticed by Boaz. I can almost hear Boaz humming "Ain't She Sweet," soon followed by a rousing duet of "Happy Days Are Here Again."

Ruth's journey to the grain fields had been an arduous one. After being left a young childless widow, she moved to a faraway land to serve her grieving mother-in-law, Naomi. Ruth suffered the loss of her husband, her home, her family members, and her culture. That is a lot of loss. She certainly deserved a break. Who would have blamed Ruth if her theme song had become "Born to Lose"? Instead, we hear her heart sing, "I Will Follow You."

"I Will Follow You" was also Habakkuk's song. Well, he eventually sang that joyous melody. We don't know a lot about Habakkuk, but we do know he began where most of us do—with the well-worn words every disillusioned mind has sung: "Why me?" "Why this?" "Why now?" When he stopped complaining, took a break, and began to praise, Habakkuk wrote one of the most beautiful prayers ever set to music. Listen to a few of the lines and feel free to tap your toe and shout your praise:

> Though the fig tree should not blossom, and there be no fruit on the vines, though the yield of the olive should fail, and the fields produce no food,

though the flock should be cut off from the fold, and there be no cattle in the stalls, yet I will exult in the LORD, I will rejoice in the God of my salvation. The Lord GOD is my strength, and He has made my feet like hinds' feet, and makes me walk on my high places.

HABAKKUK 3:17–19 NASB

This prayer/song, which never fails to move me, exposes the heart of a man who went from rags to riches spiritually. Habakkuk discovered that, even if his crops and flocks failed, he would still have reason to rejoice. I've been there too. I fretted in lean years about our crops (groceries) and our flock (family). And I too discovered that "His Name Is Wonderful," regardless of stormy seasons and slim pickins.

Do you have a theme song that others hear when they listen to your life? What title would you give it? Would your family agree?

Dear Lord Jesus, some of us need to sing a new song. Will you teach us the words? Help us to sing in harmony with the Holy Spirit so our song will delight your heart. Amen.

Risky Living

[Peter] cried out, "Lord, save me!"
Immediately Jesus reached out his hand and caught him.
MATTHEW 14:30–31

My husband led a high-risk childhood. He was wild and a risk-taker: you know, the type you pray doesn't move in next door. He was raised in Gay, Michigan (no, I didn't make that up). Les, his four brothers, and sister, Diane, lived in their small town (population one hundred) nine hundred yards from Lake Superior. In the winter they averaged two hundred inches of snow — although it wasn't unusual to have three and even four hundred inches in one season. We can only imagine the snow adventures that created.

One winter when Les was about ten years old, he and some friends were breaking snowdrifts off cliffs. They would walk out as close to the cliff's edge as they dared and then kick until the drift would break off and tumble to the ground twenty-five feet below. Once Les misjudged the edge and tumbled headlong to the ground below. The large accumulation of snow softened his landing, but the broken snowdrift followed Les. In seconds the only sign of him was two feet sticking out, and they were kicking. His friends scrambled to his rescue, digging him out with their hands.

Now that's enough to leave a permanent set of chill bumps on a kid and on his mother (if she ever found out). Some risks aren't worth taking. Like bear tampering . . .

One of Les's childhood diversions was to throw rocks at bears while they were dining at the dump. (Call me cautious, but I wouldn't have the starch to throw a rock at a bear if it was stuffed and mounted, much less if it was breathing.) When the bears became agitated, they would chase the kids up a hill until the children were out of sight. Believing they were rid of their tormentors, the bears would return to the dump only to have these daring imps reappear.

One time Les was visiting his cousins, and they decided to stir up some bear fur—only these annoyed bears became ticked. The boys ran until their hearts were in their mouths and still the bears were in hot pursuit. All parties involved were thinking about the fellows becoming the third course of a seventeen-course meal. But of course, since I'm married to Les, you can guess that he narrowly escaped, as did his cousins.

Les did decide that, after his brush with Smokey and the bandits, he wouldn't bug any more bears. Some risks aren't worth taking.

My friend Connie told me that when her husband of many years decided he wanted to be a free agent and play the field, she was devastated. She had just purchased a business, and with it came considerable financial responsibility. Reeling from the divorce and feeling financially overwhelmed, she was taken even further aback by an additional business offer. She was given an opportunity to become a partner in a building. Normally guarded, Connie was not one to wade beyond the safety of the shore. But with knees knocking and realizing she was at risk of losing every cent she had for her future,

Connie took the plunge. She confessed it was the scariest thing she had ever done.

That was four years ago. Today she not only has a thriving business but also the building she invested in is one of the loveliest in our town. Connie learned that some risks are worth taking.

That's the problem with risks: some are worth taking, some aren't. Some of the risks I've taken that turned out poorly have been the greatest teachers for making good future choices. And some sure-shot risks have been long-term detrimental. Hmm, this is complex. Bad could be good, good could be miserable, bad could be disabling, and good could turn out great. I guess that's why it's called a risk.

I'm really not one to dive headlong into life, but I don't want to miss the wave and be left high and dry on the shore. I wonder if that's how Peter felt when he stepped from the boat's safety to join Jesus in the raging sea (Matt. 14:28–32). Peter wanted to take the risk, but then he focused on the storm and began to sink. Stepping on the water wasn't risky for Peter because he was walking toward Jesus. No, the big risk was taking his eyes off the Lord and being overwhelmed by his circumstances. Even then the Lord extended a helping hand.

That's the safety factor in facing life's risks: Jesus. If you are walking toward him to the best of your ability, he will see you through life's unpredictable waters—but you must risk launching the boat. Just ask Peter or Connie.

Lord, what a risk you took loving us. Give us the wisdom and courage to risk loving you in return. Amen.

Sign on the Dotted Line

Since we have gifts that differ according to the grace
given to us, let each exercise them accordingly.
ROMANS 12:6 NASB

Risky behavior at this juncture in my life is wearing lace on my flannels and adding a jigger of orange juice to my Maalox. Although recently . . .

I signed on the dotted line to take a watercolor class with my friend Carol. A truly radical move. I'm a wanna-be artist whereas Carol *is* an artist. Even when we were kids Carol carried an easel while I carried an eraser. Carol's scribbles looked like Monet's while my finest effort had a curious resemblance to scribbles.

Through the years Carol has continued to develop in her artistic endeavors while I have continued to yearn. I have found that to yearn and to learn are quite different. One takes much less effort and a lot less risk than the other.

One day Carol mentioned she wanted to take a water-color class at a local art store. She was reluctant to sign up because she didn't want to attend alone. That was when I heard myself say, "I'll take the class with you." (This wasn't one of those out-of-body experiences; it was an out-of-my-mind response.) "You will?" she said incredu-lously. "Yes," I answered, sounding as surprised as she looked.

During opening introductions in the first class, I knew I was in trouble. All the participants had prior art training—except me. (I decided the time I tripped over and spilled a can of paint on the porch probably wouldn't count.)

After the introductions, we moved into the opening exercises, which were designed to free us up and show us how watercolors moved and mixed. While the other students giggled and delighted in their lovely results, I had become bonded to my brush. I couldn't seem to cast my brush lavishly across the paper like the others. Instead, I made microscopic movements, as if the sable brush was cemented to my hand.

How one could be intimidated by a brush, a piece of paper, and some colors is beyond me, but I obviously was. The teacher kept taking my hand and forcing it across the paper in an attempt to limber me up. But as soon as she let go, I regressed to quarter-inch strokes. At the close of class she announced that the group was to do some artsy homework while I, who had to have the brush pried from my curled fingers, was told to practice moving my brush back and forth across an empty sheet of paper.

See Patsy. See Patsy's brush. See Patsy choke her brush.

The following week continued to be painful. I was the only one who didn't seem to grasp what we were doing. Duh. I thought about quitting, but I hate defeat (almost as much as humiliation). We tried different experiments with the wet paint such as sprinkling salt into it. This caused the paint to create soft shooting flares of color, adding a lovely dimension to the pictures. Well, actually mine looked more like ... well ... like globs of salt sitting in wet paint. I just didn't seem to have the gift.

Week after challenging week I wanted to quit but then told myself I was probably on the brink of Monetism. So

I hung in there. I made it through the final class but no breakthrough broke through my lackluster performance. My pictures were a sight; some were a blur and a couple resembled images of birds, but we weren't sure if they were living or deceased.

Then it happened. I decided in the privacy of my home to attempt to put into practice some of the insights the teacher had shared. Before my eyes some flowers began to emerge, and it almost frightened me. I wasn't used to identifiable results; it was rather jolting.

Later that day Carol dropped by, and I cautiously slipped out my painting for her perusal. She remained speechless for some time. Then, regaining her voice, she whispered, "Patsy, this is good."

I knew it, I knew it. I would soon be on tour showing my pictures throughout the land. No, make that the world. Well, as soon as that nauseous wave of fame passed, reality settled in. Carol and I decided we should frame my flowers fast lest they wilt, and I lose my only proof of being an artist.

Carol and I concluded there are two types of artists. There are those who are artists by gift and those who are artists by guts. We know which one I am.

Now, how about you? Are you willing to take a risk (even if you're not the best in the field) and learn (not yearn for) a new skill, set a new goal, or help a dream come true? If so, please sign on the dotted line.

Thank you, Lord Creator, that because of who you are, we can be more than we ever imagined. Amen.

Fancy Footwork

In the name of Jesus Christ of Nazareth, walk.
ACTS 3:6

I hate being stuck, don't you? Like in traffic jams where, by the time the traffic clears, you have become executor of the estate for your newfound friends in the car next to you. Or stuck in a checkout lane because an item isn't marked and the teller has to wire Taiwan for a price check. How about the times you get stuck in a conversation with salespeople, an angry boss, or someone who just is a hopeless prattler. If that's not bad enough, have you ever been superglued to something? Now, honey, that's stuck. (My friend, in an attempt to do a fast repair on her earring, superglued her finger to her earlobe.)

Life is full of stuck possibilities. In fact, when you think about it, we are kind of stuck here on planet earth until further notice. Or, as my hymnal puts it, "Till the Roll Is Called Up Yonder." Makes me think we better make the best out of stuck lest life turn into one big rut.

I hate ruts. They're so ... so rutlike. Ruts are common, unimaginative, and oh, so boring. I know because I've spent time in them. Actually, I even took up emotional residence in a couple. To make them comfortable (I planned on staying), I even decorated them. I adorned the walls with excuses: "I can't," "I tried," and "I don't wanna." Those were just a few of the plagues, I mean plaques, I hung in my ruts.

Instead of "Welcome," my doormat stated, "Enter at Your Own Risk." You see, rut-dwellers tend to be irksome and dreary. Besides, ruts are personal, and normally it's only one to a rut. The rut-ee, if crowded, could growl, and like a sleeping dog, it is best to let the person lie.

I can usually spot a rut-dweller from twenty paces (takes one to know one). They lack luster, imagination, energy, and interest. They tend to slurp, slump, and sleep a lot. They prefer to gripe rather than grow, and they enjoy whine with their candlelight.

Who really wants to be like that? I saw that hand! No, you don't. In your heart of hearts (does that mean we have two?), you know ruts offer no future. At least not one with sparkle, celebration, and verve. Let's rid our lives of ruts even if we have to excavate to find our way out.

Have you ever observed excavators? First thing they do is send out surveyors to assess. This is where the Holy Spirit and several of your wise friends (not other rut-dwellers) can assist. The Holy Spirit can reveal to you why you are stuck, and he can empower you to change (although he won't usually do all the work without your involvement). Your friends can help strengthen your resolve and pray for you in the process. Solomon informs us of the value of team participation: "Two are better than one . . . If one falls down [into a rut], his friend can help him up" (Eccl. 4:9–10).

After the surveyors comes the heavy equipment to break up the hard stuff. Hmm, like our heads? Or perhaps our hearts. "And I shall take the heart of stone out of their flesh and give them a heart of flesh, that they may walk in My statutes and keep My ordinances, and do them" (Ezek. 11:19–20 NASB).

To walk in his ways is our goal. His ways rescue us from our rut-dwelling ways. Because ruts have limited walking space, rut-dwellers are more into sitting, remoteing, and molding rather than moving. Whereas when we walk in his ways, they are challenging, enlightening, and adventuresome.

My mom is eighty-one, and she's proud of it. In the past few years of her life she has become a walker. Every day she heads out for a hike. Sometimes it's just laps around her circular driveway, but she keeps those size-four feet a-movin'. Mom's determined no mold will grow in her socks. Recently she went to a podiatrist, and the doctor was impressed with how healthy her feet are. I'm sure a portion of her fancy footwork is due to all the walking she does.

Now just imagine what might happen if we were to step out of our old routine and deliberately walk in his ways. Why, we might even do a little break dancing on our way up and out of that hard place.

C'mon, sister rut-dwellers, boogie out of there. Risk life!

Jesus, you lead; I want to follow. Amen.

Heavenbound

Now we know that if the earthly tent we live in is destroyed,
we have a building from God, an eternal house in heaven,
not built by human hands.

2 CORINTHIANS 5:1

I'm enthralled with books that have great opening lines. Oh, sure, the rest of the book must strike a flame, but a sizzling opener sparks my interest. One of my all-time favorites is a book extract from 1909 by Mark Twain entitled "Captain Stormfield's Visit to Heaven." The opening line reads, "Well, when I had been dead about thirty years, I began to get a little anxious."

When I read that line, I was hooked. I laughed aloud and then wanted to know what was going on in this story. It seems Captain Stormfield had died and was hurled immediately outside of earth's orbit, spinning through space headed for heaven. The journey was taking a smidgen longer (thirty years) than he had anticipated. I actually became lost in my attempts to stay with the Captain's journey, but I never forgot that zinger of an opening line.

Imagine being outside of our earthly orbit free-floating toward the celestial shore. Whee! It sounds delicious. Sort of how I felt as a little girl when I would swing a little too high and my tummy would be tickled by a swarm of fluttering butterflies. Very exciting, plus some. To be

Jesus-bound will be heavenly, but for now we remain on terra firma. This means that learning to stay in our own orbit is essential.

Hurling through space is one thing; hurling through life could be catastrophic. Hurling suggests we thrust ourselves forward regardless of anything or anyone in our path.

Consider the disciple, orbital Peter, a fellow who had trouble keeping his feet on solid ground. He was always flinging himself into thin air. Remember when Jesus was arrested and Peter hurled himself toward the guard, rearranging the guard's anatomy with his sword? Jesus, knowing Peter was outside of his orbit, stepped in and healed the astonished guard. Peter, despite his good intentions, wasn't helping the situation or Jesus.

When we step out of our orbit into someone else's, we don't help either. Knowing when to stay back and when to step forward can be a hard call if we don't have well-defined boundaries. I'm sure Peter thought he was doing the right — even the valiant — thing. But he wasn't.

I'm a Peter. At least in the sense that I've stepped, sometimes rushed, and yes, even hurled myself into others' orbits. Even lopped off a few ears (at least it probably felt like it to those involved). In fact, I remember far too clearly a situation some years ago where I felt led (ugh) to inform (even though she had not asked) a dear woman of some of her character flaws. She was gracious even though I had hurled myself into her orbit uninvited. This event still brings me pain as I recall it. I have prayed that Jesus intervene on her behalf and heal that unnecessary wound I inflicted.

I know the Lord has forgiven me, but I don't want him to release me from the regret I feel. It serves as a sort of orbital monitoring device keeping me in my designated space. For I have found there is plenty for me to do in my own solar system without attempting adjustments in someone else's.

Do you remember the television show from the 1970s called *Lost in Space?* On board the spaceship was a shallow, self-consumed professor whom everyone in the TV audience loved to hate. He exemplified all of our worst traits, always causing a stir and blundering his way through everyone else's orbits.

We too become offensive when we lack wisdom, sensitivity, and good judgment toward those around us. We need to respect others' space and clean up our own orbit. Then, one day, one glorious day, in the twinkling of an eye, we will be out of here — not lost in space, but headed through space toward Home!

Thank you, Lord, that we are glory bound. Hallelujah!

"However, Lord"

Be it done to me according to your word.
LUKE 1:38 NASB

When Les asks me where I want to eat, I often will say, "I don't care, wherever." Then he will say, "What about the Inn?"

My immediate reply is, "No, I don't want to go there. Anywhere but there."

"Okay," he will respond, "then how about the Fiesta?"

"No, not the Inn or the Fiesta, but anywhere else."

By now we both know I didn't really mean "wherever," and it will shorten the process if I just tell him where I'm willing to go.

I have had this same conversation with the Lord. I tell him in prayer I will do whatever he asks of me. Then he sends some rascals into my life, and I'm irritated. When I said "whatever," I guess I meant as long as it's not too inconvenient, not too disruptive to my schedule, and not too long-term costly. The truth is, my "Whatever, Lord" is really more a "However, Lord." "I'll do it, Lord; however, could you make it another time, a little easier, a more agreeable person, and to my liking?" I think the true "Whatever, Lord" usually comes after we have exhausted all our bright ideas, we are spent, and we have finally moved to a point of relinquishment.

Scripture gives us some beautiful examples of "Whatever, Lord" people who didn't add howevers and didn't have to come to their wit's end to trust him explicitly.

Consider the Virgin Mary's response to the angel's visitation. A maiden with her whole life before her is asked to risk scandal, misunderstanding, lunacy charges, and possibly stoning. Mary, however, doesn't see it as a risk but as an honor to be chosen (even if it included scandal, misunderstanding, and so forth). We read her powerful "Whatever, Lord" in the gospel of Luke: "Behold, the bondslave of the Lord; be it done to me according to your word" (Luke 1:38 NASB).

Now that's trust. How impressive that such a young woman would respond immediately to a request never before made of anyone. It wasn't as if others had ever been in this situation and Mary could use their experience to guide her. When the angel Gabriel extended God's incredible invitation, Mary was flying solo with no previous experience. She also was so-low in her response, for Scripture tells us her heart was humble.

Mary's reply surfaces another insight about a "Whatever, Lord" person: that individual has humility. Relinquishment (when I give up on me and give in to him) and humility (lowliness of mind) are rare attributes. It almost sounds as if these two qualities depend on each other, doesn't it? Like you can't have one without the other? But wait, there's more . . .

Remember Abigail? She was the wife of Nabal, a hard-hearted man who had no respect for authority. Nabal's arrogance and his unwillingness to extend gratitude to others placed Abigail, her family, and their workers' lives in jeopardy. David and his men had protected Nabal's shepherds and sheep from vandals. But when David asked if he and his men could share in the festivities of a feast day with Nabal, he rebuffed David. Abigail rushed to meet David, who had sharpened his sword in preparation to repay Nabal for his unneighborly attitude, and in an act of relinquishment and humility she presented her case. David was moved by this woman's passion to right wrongs and to protect him from making a foolish mistake. He not only honored her request to spare her household, but also, after the (natural) death of her husband, David made Abigail his wife. Her zealous entreaty, laced with humility and relinquishment, is found in 1 Samuel 25 and worth feasting your eyes on.

So we add passion to our "Whatever, Lord" list — passion to do what is honorable and therefore right in God's eyes. We "see" and hear Abigail's passion when she dismounts her donkey in David's presence, falls on her face before him, and says, "My lord, let the blame be on me alone" (1 Sam. 25:24).

Abigail's salutation disarmed David. I'm sure he anticipated a defensive attitude — one full of excuses from a scoundrel whom he did not plan to listen to. Instead, David comes upon a "Whatever, Lord" woman, an honorable woman with an impassioned plea. Rather than a whiny, self-centered request, Abigail demonstrates, by laying her life on the line, a warm concern for the welfare of all.

Relinquishment, humility, and passion: "A cord of three strands is not quickly broken" (Eccl. 4:12).

Are you a "whatever" woman or a "however" woman?

How do you exhibit godly passion?

Who presents a picture of humility you can emulate?

What does the Lord want you to relinquish to him?

Jesus, "Whatever, Lord" is a scary prayer; yet we want to trust you, and so we risk . . . Whatever, Lord. Amen.

Where Are You?

Jesus Christ is the same yesterday and today and forever.
HEBREWS 13:8

A woman recently wrote to me asking, "How does one find God?" Hmm. Great question, isn't it? God is sort of like the wind in that we see evidence of his presence; yet he isn't easily grasped. We can't touch him, yet we can feel his presence as surely as our own. We don't hear an audible voice, yet at times he speaks as definitely and clearly as anyone we've heard.

I see God's fingerprints in his handiwork: a sunrise, a shooting star, a lilac bush, and a newborn's smile. I observe a measure of his strength in a hurricane, an earthquake, a thunderbolt. I see his creativity in a kangaroo, the Grand Canyon, and a blue-eyed, redheaded baby. I detect his humor in a porpoise, a cactus, and a two-year-old's twinkling eyes. I am aware of his mysteriousness when I consider the Trinity, the solar system, and his desire to be in communion with us. "What is man that you are mindful of him?" (Ps. 8:4).

But how do we find God? Sometimes we search him out, and sometimes he "finds" us. Every time we think of God it is because he first had us on his mind. The Lord is always the initiator. He has been from the beginning (Gen. 1:1), and he will be to the end (Rev. 1:7). So know that once you have invited him to enter your life, you are on his mind and he is in your heart.

The Lord settled into our hearts is another mystery. How could we, with our tiny hearts — not to mention our itsy-bitsy brains — house him who is without beginning or end (Rev. 1:8)? We could not — aside from his miraculous power and his desire to inhabit us.

I have learned that sometimes we will be aware of his closeness and sometimes we won't. At times we experience the sweetness of God's nearness and at other times the frightening loneliness of his distance. The Lord hasn't changed locations, but we might have become caught up in our own agendas and forgotten his presence and availability. Other times the Lord will be silently still (scary) for holy purposes (awesome) we don't understand (frustrating), yet . . . (hallelujah).

How does one find God? Perhaps we need to rest from our pursuit of the Almighty and allow him to reveal himself to us. This is not to say we should stop any honorable efforts to find him such as in church, Bible study, or fellowship. On the contrary, these endeavors shore us up while we wait. But in the midst of our journey, we need to allow him to lead us even to lonely terrain. Surprisingly, our loneliness can cause us to pursue the Lord even more.

How does one find God? He is in our prayers guiding our words, he is in our songs as we worship him, and he is filling our mouths when we comfort a friend or speak wisdom to someone who needs hope. Sometimes we search so hard for the miraculous that we miss the obvious reality of his ever-present nearness. Count your blessings. He is in them too.

We can't command the Lord into our awareness. He is King; we are his beloved subjects. When our hearts are tenderly responsive ("Whatever, Lord") and it suits his greater plan, then the Lord will lift the thin veil that separates us. And we will be stunned to realize that he has been closer than our own breath all along.

By the way, it has been my experience that I keep refinding him, which has helped to define me. You too may lose track of your faith. Remember, it is never too late to step back on the path.

Lord who fills the universe and longs to fill me, please enter my life with your fullness. I long to experience your closeness, but I also will not shun your silence; for you are faithful to continue your work in both. May I be faithful in return, and may my prayer to you always be "Whatever, Lord." Amen.

Yep, That's Me!

The LORD does not look at the things man looks at.
Man looks at the outward appearance,
but the LORD looks at the heart.

1 SAMUEL 16:7

I dashed into the local market, picked up some milk, bread, and a few goodies, and then made my way to the express checkout. The cashier looked at me and asked, "Now, don't you get a discount today?"

"No," I mumbled, wondering what she meant. She rang up my items while I puzzled over her query. I had glanced through our town newspaper earlier, and I couldn't recollect seeing any coupons. Maybe she thought I worked there and qualified for a discount.

Then suddenly it hit me like a ton of face cream: She thought I was a senior.

"Excuse me, but how would one qualify for the discount?" I asked in a syrupy tone of voice.

She looked up and sweetly replied, "Oh, this is senior citizens' day for those over sixty."

That she could even consider me more than sixty years of age when I'm a mere fifty-one was disheartening. Not a news flash, just another older-than-you-look affirmation. If I had saved every old-age comment made to me through the years and if they were as valuable as, say, old comic books, I'd be sippin' soda under a palm tree on my own island.

I really believe we are a people hung up on our hormones and hairdos, but c'mon girls, none of us wants to wither before her time. Actually, I think this ancient countenance of mine is my grandmother's fault; she always looked centuries older than she was. When I was a child I was certain only Methuselah was older than my grandma. Yet she lived on for decades, bless her orthopedic heart.

Do you think, if we could get past our looks, we would be deeper people? I admit I like to look good. I take delight in developing a pleasing wardrobe. I enjoy compliments on my appearance. Yet even more meaningful is when someone tells me she enjoys my work. Or that the Lord has used me to open her eyes in some area of her life and encouraged her growth. Or that I brought her a smile in the midst of hard times. In fact, those kinds of comments actually make me feel . . . well . . . pretty.

I've also noticed that when I feel good about myself I seem to get more compliments about how I look. Do you think the condition of our heart and mind-set impacts our looks? I'm certain attitudes do.

I saw a young woman the other day who was wearing her 'tude like a tunic. She was wrapped up in herself and was looking for someone to vent on. I'm almost certain if she had dropped her attitude she would have been quite attractive, but what was visible was an angry, hostile countenance.

One way to defuse hostility is to accept ourselves. There is nothing more churning than to be in a constant tirade with the mirror. Not only does it discourage us, but it also sets us up for jealousy toward others, which adds to our anger. When we lighten up and learn to accept — and even appreciate — our looks, it relieves inner tension and others find us more attractive as well. Acceptance is a great way to achieve a face-lift.

Speaking of needing a face-lift ... Think of the worst picture you have ever had taken of you. Now imagine someone enlarging it and sending it out to thousands of people without your knowledge. How would you feel?

I can tell you how I felt because that happened to me. I was surprised, hurt, embarrassed—and then I got over it. My husband often tells me when things don't go well: "Worse things happen in better families." In other words, *Don't sweat the small stuff.* Besides, even though it was a poor picture, when I saw it I had to admit, "Yep, that's me!"

Our looks are important because they are part of our uniqueness. They are proof we are one of a kind. So we need to appreciate our appearance but not idolize it. In the end, it won't be how we looked but how we loved that will matter.

Lord, today as I fuss over my hair, my makeup, my clothes, help me to remember the makeover you started in me when we first became acquainted. And remind me to be willing to submit to any reworking you wish to undertake now. Amen.

Cracked Pots and Tarnished Vessels

But we have this treasure in earthen vessels,
that the surpassing greatness of the power may be
of God and not from ourselves.

2 CORINTHIANS 4:7 NASB

I attended a gala occasion recently to which I wore a dressy pants outfit with stylish heels. My hair was fluffed, and my ears were adorned with a new pair of dazzling earrings. I felt spiffy . . . until I arrived at the event. I was the only woman with slacks on, and I felt awkward. After a considerable time I spotted another gal in slacks, and I wondered if she would want to sit with me and be best friends. Soon several others arrived in similar attire, and I no longer felt the need to bond.

Aren't we funny? We work hard to be originals and then fear our originality has made us different. I enjoy being center stage unless it's under a critical spotlight. Like the time I spoke only to learn afterward that my slip was hanging in a southerly direction waving to the onlookers. Following the session, several hundred women alerted me so I could hike it up. Believe me, I wanted to take a hike . . . an exceedingly long one to another land. Despite today's fads I prefer to keep my underwear undercover. Know what I mean?

Even though this blooper was embarrassing, I have lived long enough to understand that none of us has a corner on blunders. We are not one of a kind when it comes to gumming up the works; that's a human condition we all share. But we are exclusive in our mix of personalities, backgrounds, relationships, callings, and life choices. This means we are both like and unlike others.

I've noticed the people who seem most at home with themselves are not rocked by their faux pas. They are able to move past their flub-ups without remaining devastated or absorbing them into their sense of worth. I admire that since I used to be Ms. Flip-Out. The more I flitted and fought against my humanity the more flubs I seemed to make and the worse I felt. I was emotionally in a stir. Gradually I gave up my attempts to be something I wasn't (perfect), which made it possible for me to be more comfortable with who I am (a one-of-a-kind cracked pot).

Of course, some days I fall back into old patterns. Then I have to be reminded by other flawed, yet one-of-a-kind vessels of my freedom in Christ.

Speaking of flawed, I guess we could say Jonah the prophet was a fishy vessel. His calling was to be a landlubber, but instead he headed for the deep blue sea. Jonah sprung a leak and sunk in over his head before he realized his error and finally agreed to fulfill his one-of-a-kind calling by high-stepping it over to Nineveh to stand alone.

It's not easy to stand alone, and it certainly is a test of our willingness to be a one-of-a-kind-er. Ask Eve. She was an earthen vessel in the truest form, a one-and-only woman if ever there was one. Unable or unwilling to resist the enemy's fruity fling, she lost the sweetness of her highest calling.

It would seem that standing alone would take stamina, determination, and discipline. Uh-oh, these aren't my majors. Unless you count willfulness. No, wait, that's what cost Eve Paradise. Even though Eve was unique, her sin made her common . . . as does ours.

Sin tarnishes our one-of-a-kind brilliance. I have a copper pot that quickly dulls when not tended to. It has to be cleaned and polished regularly. We also lose our individual luster and become no more than common pots when we are tainted by sinful behavior.

King David, a royal pot with a deadly plot, marred his regal rank when he went for a dish on the side. His sinful actions to steal another man's wife and murder her husband robbed him of his one-of-a-kind reputation. Sin is both costly and cheap.

I've observed men and women with powerful callings diminish their one-of-a-kind effectiveness by heading out in wrong directions, making poor choices, and wanting what isn't theirs. And here's the kicker: We are all susceptible to behaving commonly and missing our individual best. All we cracked pots and tarnished vessels need to heed the lessons of Jonah, Eve, and David, and strive toward keeping our individual containers shipshape.

Dear Jesus, help us to be comfortable, not with sin, but with your one-of-a-kind design for us. We want to be our sparkling best, but we will need your cleansing protection, for we are willful. Thank you for pursuing Jonah until he followed you, for allowing Eve to experience fruit from her womb rather than just the fruit of her sin, and for graciously receiving King David when he sought your forgiveness. This gives all of us tarnished pots hope. Amen.

A Number-Ten Friend

A friend loves at all times.
PROVERBS 17:17

riendship is a word full of growth potential. One can become bigger (as in character enlargement) or one can become smaller (as in narrow-minded). Becoming a good friend is aerobic in that it takes time and effort. We don't just wake up one day, and voilà: we are Wonder Friend! The need for companionship is built into our genes, but we don't come with the know-how to be a comrade. That is learned through giving, taking, forgiving, sharing, praying, and empathizing.

Most of us feel we know what it takes to be a good friend. Yet, if that's true, why do we have so many lonely people who long for meaningful friendships? Perhaps too many of us are wanting someone to be our friend instead of being someone's friend ourselves. Also, it's easy to make mistakes in relationships. I know I've certainly flubbed up enough times. Maybe you feel that way too. In fact, let's take a gander at "Twelve Ways to Insure a Small Repertoire of Friends":

1. Breed pettiness.
2. Campaign against your friend's mate.
3. Drop in frequently.
4. Offer unsolicited advice.

5. Create opportunities to whine.
6. Nitpick their children.
7. Besiege her with phone calls.
8. Critique her decisions.
9. Encourage dissension.
10. Share freely in all her possessions.
11. Snub her other friends.
12. Insist on being her best friend.

Any of those ring a bell? They are surefire ways to remain lonely.

So, what does it take to have healthy, warm relationships? Let's peer at what makes a priceless friend. We will call it, "Twelve Ways to Be a Number-Ten Friend."

1. Believe the best.
2. Respect and set boundaries.
3. Express humor to release joy (not venom).
4. Applaud successes.
5. Maintain good manners.
6. Draw a generous friendship circle.
7. Give without expectations.
8. Praise genuinely (no gushing).
9. Support her frailty (no indulging).
10. Protect private information.
11. Pray fervently.
12. Love Jesus passionately.

Remember to leave room in your friendships for failure; otherwise, when people let you down (which they will), you will have to replace them. How exhausting. Besides, I've learned some of my most revealing lessons about myself while working through conflict.

My feelings used to get hurt much more easily than they do today. What a relief to have greater resiliency.

Also, I've learned that when I don't enter into my friends' successes with joy, it's usually because I'm jealous. Ouch, that's painful to confess ... even to myself. Jealousy is like a spider's web. It's difficult to see its slender fibers, easy to get entangled in, and hard to brush off.

The last piece of friendship advice—to love Jesus passionately—is the best counsel of all. When Jesus is our best friend, we won't approach human friendships from such a fragile place and turn people off by our consuming neediness. Jesus longs to be our Need Meeter. When we turn to him first and then turn to others, we will be better prepared to give and receive relationally and rationally.

Friendship is such an honor, our lives intersecting with others in meaningful ways. This makes friendship a joy break of the finest kind!

Lord, let's do lunch, just the two of us. ... We'll talk. Amen.

Sistership

Be devoted to one another in brotherly love.
Honor one another above yourselves.
ROMANS 12:10

Friendship is the ship the Lord often launches to keep my boat afloat. I seem to require people in my life. Scads of them. I am not the type who wants to be an island unto myself. (Unless it's Gilligan's Island.) Not that I don't want to be alone; my alone times are precious to me. I guard them and find solitude necessary for my sanity (well, what's left of it). Yet interacting with others encourages, nurtures, challenges, hones, and helps refine me. My journey has been made more joyous by connecting with friends.

One of my favorite dots in my network of friends is Carol. We are friends with history. We go back to the days when gumdrops were the latest rage in shoes. (Anyone remember those? They were a jazzed-up version of saddle shoes.)

Carol and I still tell each other secrets and giggle over our silly flaws. We know the worst about each other and choose to believe the best. We have not always known how to do that. Then Jesus entered our lives and our friendship. He taught us important skills in esteeming one another. In our thirty-nine years of relationship, we have never not been friends; but since we met the

Lord, our friendship has deepened in appreciation and affection.

We love to shop, decorate, antique, travel, dream, and scheme with each other. We have gone through the best of times in our families and the worst of times. We have celebrated and sorrowed together. We have guffawed and groaned. We have worshiped the Lord at the same church and studied the Scriptures in our homes. We have at times let the other one down, which gave us opportunity to learn the imperative friendship skill of forgiveness.

Even though we share many interests, we are opposite personalities. I am boisterous; Carol is reticent. I'm a right-now person; she's an I-can-wait gal. Even physically we are opposites. She towers over my pudgy frame. Her hair is wispy and straight while mine is bushy and frizzy. Differences and similarities along with years of caring and sharing have enhanced our sistership.

Just three weeks ago I moved. I moved only seven blocks, but I still had to pick up everything and find a place to set it down in my new abode—that or have an enormous (thirty-four years' worth of stuff) yard sale. Thankfully, I had dear friends come to my rescue and help me pack.

After arriving in our new home, I was overwhelmed at the prospect of settling in. I had thought I would pull it together rapidly. Instead, I roamed from room to room trying to remember my name. Carol came to give support (and to verify my identity) every morning for four days. She assisted me until early evening, when she would then make our dinner, serve us, and clean up. You can only guess what a gift that was to me emotionally. I never expected that kind of beyond-the-call-of-duty effort, but I'm certain our new home ownership would have found me sinking before I could even unload the cargo, if it were not for Carol's life preserver of kindness.

What is it about moving that is so disassembling? The leaving of the old? The adjusting to the new? The disheveling of all our stuff? The initial sense of unconnectedness? Or all of the above? Carol's and my long-term connectedness served as a stabilizer during this turbulent time. And it was great to have someone with similar tastes to bounce ideas off of about furniture placement, window treatments, and picture arrangements.

By evening, when my wagon was draggin', Carol would catch her second wind and perform wonders in the kitchen. This girl can cook! Every night her feast renewed our strength and our determination to get back at it. The following day we would eat the leftovers for lunch, and in the evening she would prepare yet another culinary delight.

I'm thankful that the Lord knew we would need each other to survive various storms — and that he made available the harbor of friendship.

Thank you, Lord, that you haven't left me to dog-paddle through life's waterspouts all alone. Amen.

God's Instruments

Since my youth, O God, you have taught me,
and to this day I declare your marvelous deeds.

PSALM 71:17

Have you noticed some peculiar quack-ups in Scripture? No, not people, but things that behaved . . . well
. . . rather oddly. For instance, Balaam's talking donkey.
The only donkey I ever heard chatter was Frances the
Talking Mule in the movies, and she (or is it he?) definitely had the benefit of technological intervention.

No doubt Balaam, the rider, was startled when the
donkey began to converse, although Balaam continued
the conversation without missing a beat (see Num.
22:29). Scripture tells us the Lord opened the donkey's
mouth and he (the donkey) said to Balaam, "What have I
done to you, that you have struck me these three times?"
(Num. 22:28 NASB). I wonder if our animals have some
things on their mind they would like to say to us. If your
pet's mouth were opened, what do you think he would
proclaim? Perhaps, "What's with the doggie treats? They
taste like Styrofoam!" Or, "Call an exterminator; I'm not
catching one more mouse in this rat trap." Or maybe,
"You haven't cleaned my cage in a week, and you call *me*
a birdbrain!" The possibilities are endless. I'm sort of glad
they are semi-silent . . . for now.

Anyway, back to oddities. I've always thought it strange that the little boy's lunch box (John 6:9–14) turned into a cafeteria for thousands with leftovers. Now there's a lunch that smacks of entrepreneurial possibilities. I bet the Colonel would like to get hold of that recipe.

Or what about the bowl of flour and the jar of oil belonging to the widow who housed Elijah (1 Kings 17:10–16)? No matter how much they used, the containers of flour and oil were not exhausted until the famine was over. It was a gift that kept on giving.

Aaron's budding rod is peculiar to me as well (Num. 17:8). Here was a branch without soil, sunlight, a root system, or someone to tend it. And what happened? It became an overnight success. It budded, blossomed, and—get this—produced ripe fruit. Now compare that with my lovely poinsettia that I recently received as a gift. When it arrived, it was heady with pink and vibrant green leaves. It was thriving. After forty-eight hours in my home under my attentive care the stems were bald (as in stark naked), and the petals had been humbled to a scraggly, limp, embarrassed few. So, Aaron, any tips?

Another quirky situation was when water poured forth from a rock (Exod. 17:6). Rock is nature's strongest, most solid substance. So how did a gushing stream get in there? We aren't talking about a few pails' worth dripping out. Or even a trough full. No, we're talking Niagara Falls. Enough water billowed out to quench the thirst of thousands upon thousands of people and their herds. Whoa, talk about odd.

In that same category of out-of-the-norm events, how about an ark parked on your back forty (Gen. 6:14)? That would surely get the neighbors' goats (and their horses, chickens, and dogs too). I'll bet that ark was listed in the local newspaper under "Hiraam's Believe It or Not." This wasn't a kayak but a ship-sized vessel that covered a football field. It perched on dry land waiting for an ocean to pass by. Pretty strange.

Perchance when the water floated Noah's boat it also doused Moses' bush.

Imagine a bush aflame but never consumed by the fire (Exod. 3:2–5). Then add to that God's voice emanating out of it. That would stop me in my tracks too!

If the talking bush didn't paralyze me with wonder, I'm sure the manna would have (I'm into miraculous meals). What an odd sight it must have been: groceries falling from heaven and dropped on doorsteps. (The closest I came to manna was when I was a kid. We used to catch fresh snow in bowls on our doorstep and add vanilla and milk for our version of heavenly hash.)

The wonder of it all is that the Lord can use everything for whatever purposes he chooses. Not to mention every*one*. I'm amazed he allows a donkey to speak, but I think it's more incredible that he speaks to us at all. For most of the time we are really quite ill-mannered, if not downright stubborn. Yet he chooses oddities and odd ducks for his divine purposes.

-ᛟ-

God, help me to see the odd instruments in my life that speak of you. Help me to stay in tune with you so as not to miss any message you send my way. Amen.

That's Odd

O LORD, you have searched me and you know me . . .
you are familiar with all my ways.
PSALM 139:1, 3

The dictionary describes *odd* as "strange, unusual, or peculiar; eccentric in conduct; in excess of what is usual, regular, approximated, or expected."

I am fond of this condition called "odd" for it smacks of originality, spontaneity, and sagacity. It takes spunk and smarts not to follow the freeway but to search for what the poet Robert Frost called "the road less traveled."

When I was growing up, I wanted my parents to be "normal." Every time they acted odd I panicked. My goal as a young person was to fit in. Today I look back and celebrate my parents' oddities because they made my folks sparkle with interest and spared me the boredom and blueprint of "normal." (Besides, we all know that normal is just a setting on our dryers.)

When I was a child, I had the painful privilege of living in many homes. Some of them, though lovely, seemed strange and unusual to me. I remember one home in which my bedroom was the recreation room. I would fall asleep at night looking at the padded black and white musical notes strewn across the wall at odd angles.

In the kitchen we had colored appliances that were foreign to my eyes since everyone I knew had white ones. I remember the wallpaper was from France and had French words on it. I always wondered what that mysterious verbiage meant. The kitchen contained a built-in booth, which I thought was cozy but different (none of my friends had booths). The living room had a full wall mural that was soft and attractive, but once again outside of the norm. The carpeting was so thick and deep you could tell who had walked through the room by the size of the footprint left behind. Vacuuming was a full-time requirement to keep the carpeting fluffed and foot-less. It may have been the impetus for moving, though, for we relocated less than a year later.

The next home was about as normal as they come (a three-bedroom brick); so my mom soon became bored with it, and we packed up again. That move took us to a fascinating home a couple of miles from where we had been living. Some of the walls in this home were padded and tufted; most were covered in beautiful wood custom crafted by a carpenter for his family. The different woods created the effect of a luxury liner in some of the rooms while others reminded me of a cabin in the woods. My friends thought our home charming but odd.

Today I find odd appealing. It safeguards my chances of settling into a cookie-cutter existence without dynamic distinctives. I enjoy interviewing people and finding out what strange things they have done, places they have lived in, locales they have traveled to, and projects they have worked on. It has been enlightening and even inspiring to hear some of their answers.

One gal, who had also moved a lot, told me her family had the odd history of going repeatedly from rags to riches. Each time they lost everything they would live an opposite lifestyle until they could recoup their finances. During one of their moves back to rags, she and her mom were told they could take only three possessions with them. Her mother selected three paintings. Because of limited space in the vehicle and the long trip in front of them, her dad nailed the paintings to the inside roof of the car. There was no back seat so her dad made her a bed in the back hatch, and on their long journey she traveled staring at the lovely paintings. They lived in their car and ate little sausages out of cans. She confessed she didn't know until adulthood the oddity of their lifestyle. Her somewhat eccentric dad made the arduous trips and shifts in income a grand adventure.

My friend Mary lived in a floating, two-story house in Seattle; a missionary friend lived in a grass hut for awhile; my son's teacher had a swimming pool in the center of her home (all rooms emptied into the pool); and I met a family that lived on an island. There is no end to odd living arrangements or, for that matter, odd homeowners.

Speaking of odd living arrangements, John the Baptist lived in the desert and ate bugs (give me those little sausages any day). His parents were deceased, he wasn't married (I wonder why . . . duh), and he dressed funny. Yet Scripture refers to him as the one who came to make ready the way of the Lord (John 1:23).

Do you feel awkward because something about you is out of the norm? Maybe it's your looks, your educational status, or your family background. Why not relish your uniqueness? And then trust the One who loves the peculiar to use your life with all its odd variations.

Jesus, today remind me that no shadows or variations from the "norm" have reached me that have not first passed through your loving hands. Regardless how odd the circumstances may be, teach me to relish the abnormal and to see ways you want to use it in my life and in others' lives through me. Amen.

No Pink Duck Rides

> But ye are a chosen generation, a royal priesthood,
> an holy nation, a peculiar people; that ye should
> show forth the praises of him who hath called you
> out of darkness into his marvelous light.
>
> 1 Peter 2:9 KJV

I once read the quip, "Life ain't no ride on no pink duck." It stuck in my brain like a colorful Post-It note. I have recalled it many times for my own enjoyment as well as a reminder that life ain't easy.

One winter evening, as I walked home from my mother's apartment, a woman from Mom's building was disembarking from her car and expressed her fear of falling on the ice. I asked what I could do to help her feel safe. She suggested I take her left arm while she used her cane in her right hand. We slowly made our way across the frozen patches.

When we reached the curb, she asked, "How old are you?" I told her, and she replied wistfully, "How fortunate you are." Then she stated sadly, "But I must tell you that you don't have a lot to look forward to. Aging is painful." She turned to enter the apartment and pleasantly called out, "Happy Thanksgiving!"

Have you noticed that we are laughter and tears, dirges and dances, jubilations and consternations, hallelujahs and woes? We proclaim, "Life is dreadful" in one breath and "Happy holidays!" in the next. We have good days, great days, and way-down-deep-in-the-pit days. Some seasons are easier than others, while some are downright impossible. I've wondered how some folks have survived the many hardships that have come their way. Others' lives have seemed almost charmed. For each of us, our days are unpredictable, and we tip the scales from preposterous to precious. Life is a gift bulging with mystery, intrigue, comedy, tragedy — and purpose.

When we realize our days here matter, our pain has significance, and our choices are meaningful, we can step through the darkest of times with hope in our hearts. It's not that we won't waver, but even our inquiries have the potential, when we are seeking, to lead us to a stronger faith.

I'm certain the woman in the parking lot was right when she said aging was painful. Yet I also know that the teenage years can be traumatic (mine were). In fact, even my young-adult years were riddled with emotional and relational pain. My sons both told me their most painful school years were during junior high. Does this mean life is a pain? Sure does . . . but thankfully not all the time. Pain is not the only thread in life's tapestry.

Joy must be the shocking pink thread in our tapestry, because people seem stunned by this flamboyant stitch. When we exhibit joy during trying times, others view us as odd ducks 'cause everyone knows life ain't no ride on no pink duck.

I find that my joy is enlarged by understanding that, as a child of God, even my pain has purpose. That realization doesn't eliminate my pain, but it makes it more manageable, allowing me other emotions in the midst of calamity, including shocking pink joy.

The Lord has called us to be a peculiar people. Not strange in the sense we act bizarre, but peculiar in the ways we respond to life because the Lord's Spirit is working within us.

Remember Stephen? There was an odd duck, if ever we should see one. He was chosen from and by the congregation of the disciples to minister (Acts 6:1–6). As a man full of the Spirit, wisdom, grace, and power, he outraged men of lesser character, and they lied to eliminate him and the powerful impact he was having on others. A mob mentality flashed through the group of rage-aholics who stoned Stephen to death. In his last breaths, he called on the Lord to receive his spirit, and then, falling on his knees, this odd man said the most peculiar thing: "Lord, do not hold this sin against them" (Acts 7:60).

It's one thing to eventually forgive unjust behavior, but to ask that others not even be held accountable while one is still in the midst of excruciating, life-taking pain — why, that's downright peculiar. Make that upright peculiar. Stephen was an odd duck (not a pink duck) with a silk hat. His silk hat was the covering of the Lord over his life, which is how and why he was able to be faithful to his last breath. How comforting to read that, after he made his request, "he fell asleep" (Acts 7:60).

I know I am a strange and unusual person (many have pointed this out), but I am uncertain how often I am peculiar in an upright sense. This makes me all the more grateful for the One who offers to come alongside and assist me across the icy landscape of life.

Lord, deliver me from my strangeness and help me to become exceedingly peculiar. Amen.

Just a Minute

Wake up, O sleeper.
EPHESIANS 5:14

TICK-TOCK, TICK-TOCK. I can still hear the commanding sound of my parents' Big Ben alarm clock. TICK-TOCK. I think our neighbors heard it as well. TICK-TOCK. My dad, a milkman, could sleep through a cattle stampede, and it didn't bother him that the rafters of our house were vibrating in time to his clock's ticker. My mom was hearing impaired, so she just turned off her hearing aid at night. My ears worked fine, thank you, and every tock tended to tick me off.

It's been years since I've had to listen to the drumbeat of a Big Ben, but every once in a while I will look in a mirror, or see old friends (or worse yet, their children), or tell someone how old my children are. Then the TICK-TOCKS start to pound in my brain cells. Time seems either to be in my face or to catapult by me. It can be as elusive as my income or as contrary as my weight. Some minutes drag on for eons while some decades seem more like a fleeting dream. I don't necessarily want to harness time, but I'd like to at least corral it. I know for sure I don't want to snooze through my allotted portion.

I come from a long line of snoozers. We are firm believers in catnaps. I didn't actually hear discussions on this topic when I was growing up, but visual aids I had aplenty. My dad's napping style was definitely the best. He could sleep almost anywhere. His snoring made the Big Ben's ticks and tocks seem more like a purring kitten. Dad had little snorts in the middle of his snores, which entertained us all and sometimes startled him back to reality. Because Dad chilled easily he would form a blanket-tent for himself out of the newspaper just before drifting off. The newspaper, usually the funnies, would rise and fall with each breath, making him an amusing centerpiece in our living room. His naps were never lengthy, but his sleep was deep.

I too am a deep sleeper, but I do wake up to an alarm . . . usually alarmed. Some of my relatives, on the other hand, sleep through their wake-up calls. My son Marty could sleep through an air raid—although he's finally come up with a series of rings, buzzes, and blasts that penetrate his sleep pattern and alert him to a new day.

Speaking of multiple alarms, I once slept in a roomful of clocks (imagine the wake-up potential there). I was a guest, and the homeowner was a collector of every size clock you could imagine (minus Big Ben . . . whew!). More than fifty clocks' faces stared down on my bed. Some chimed, one cuckooed, a couple played songs, and all of them ticked and tocked in their own fascinating fashion. A couple of exceptions were part of the lineup. These were windup clocks that hadn't been wound, and for them time stood still.

Have you ever wished you could stop time to extend a precious memory, to savor the moment? I would love to have had extended time to gaze upon my newborn sons; I was so struck with their intricate beauty. If I could, I would have nestled into the moment when our first child uttered, "I love you." I wish I could have freeze-framed the tender look on my daughter-in-law Danya's face when she received her engagement ring from our son Jason. I'd like to journey back and savor the sweet moments spent with Les as we held hands and strolled Lake Superior's shores.

We can't stop time, but we can roll back the years with our memories. Hmm, I guess, in a way, memories serve as our time card, as a way to recall our days and measure our moments. Memories can tick as loud as a Big Ben clock. They can cause alarm, ring with insight, face us with truth, and even act as a wake-up call. Our yesterdays teach us how to savor our todays and tomorrows.

And we want to savor our moments now — for one day, one glorious day, we will hear the wake-up call of all wake-up calls. Not the TICK-TOCK of a Big Ben, but a big trumpet (trust me, not even snoozers will sleep through this one). Then, folks, time will be no more. We will be ushered into eternity. All time measuring devices (wristwatches, timers, sundials, grandfather clocks, alarms, stopwatches, and even the sun and moon) will be obsolete. Never again will we say, "I don't have time," "Time's running out," "How timely," "Just a minute," or "Maybe tomorrow." We will be unencumbered with time limits, and instead of savoring a memory or a moment, we will savor the Savior . . . forever.

Help us, O Lord, to squeeze out the best of every tick and tock you have allotted to us. Amen.

Fresh Starts

The blood of Jesus His Son cleanses us from all sin.

1 JOHN 1:7 NASB

Saturday night baths were a regular yet big event in my husband's family. The rotund metal tub was pulled into the center of the kitchen where the water brigade would then begin. Nippy tap water was gratefully tempered by the addition of kettles full of hot water off the crackling, wood-burning stove. When the temperature was adjusted, the bath lineup began.

The three oldest boys took their baths first—one at a time. (This was a seniority system.) Then the tub was emptied and refilled for phase two—the three youngest children. My husband, Les, was grateful, in this case, to be the middle child, which made him first for the second round in the Clairmont splashdown. The children who required assistance had a vigorous sudsing from head to toes to give them a squeaky-clean entrance into the new week.

I can only imagine the condition of the water (somewhere between mud and sludge) after child number three finished his bath. These were active children who played, fought, and worked hard in the northern woods of Michigan. How wonderful it must have felt on bath night, after a week of sponging off, to sit and soak in the tub. A savored moment to be sure. Not that they could lollygag, since they all needed a turn, and the temperature of the water was hard to maintain throughout the process. This was not a bobbing-for-apples kind of evening, but a get-down-to-business time. You can imagine, with half a dozen children to be bathed and bedded, the system needed to keep moving. By Sunday morning six well-scrubbed, well-fed, neatly attired children headed for church.

In Les's neck of the woods, they had another way, besides the Saturday night tin-tub special, of dealing with dirt: saunas. Finnish steam baths dotted Les's neighborhood. Little buildings with smokestacks on the outside and stoves full of hot rocks on the inside were the order of the day.

After disrobing in the sauna changing room (about the size of a telephone booth), you stepped into the inner room and tossed a ladle full of water onto the heated rocks. The rocks hissed in response and shot up puffs of steam that cleansed every minuscule molecule of your being. The faint of heart sat on the low benches while the hearty souls went for the top bleacher. When you left the sauna, you felt as though even your innards could pass a Good Housekeeping white-glove inspection.

I've never taken a bath in a tin tub, but I have taken a number of saunas. I left them feeling soggy, relaxed, and spanking clean. I was a low-bench participant. Cedar boughs were available on the benches to smack yourself to stimulate your blood circulation. I left that for the hearty ones. I'm not into discomfort or stinging swats, especially self-inflicted ones. (I'm more into sweets than swats. I'm your have-another-Snickers gal.)

The issue of cleanliness on this polluted planet is a constant one. Every day we shower, scrub, scrape, soak, and scour in an attempt to stay healthy and socially acceptable. In fact, I have a basket at my tubside filled with cleaning utensils: sponges, brushes, loofahs, pumice, and soaps.

As helpful as these items are, they do not compare to how clean I feel when I have spent moments in the Lord's presence, especially when I begin with a confession time. When I prayerfully remember my shortcomings, I'm not informing the Lord of anything he doesn't already know. But when I enumerate my failings, I take responsibility before him, and he then releases me from dirty shame, grimy guilt, and scummy sin. I am released from all my present tensions. I am cleansed in the innermost parts of my being where even the sauna's steam can't penetrate.

I can still picture my mom using a washboard to deal with tough stains on my dad's work clothes. Our heavenly Father doesn't have to haul out a washboard when he sees our stubbornly stained hearts. We enter the inner room when we plead the blood of Jesus, and our filthy sins become as white as snow in his presence (and that, my friends, is better than a Good Housekeeping seal of approval).

So willingly hop into his tin tub for a vigorous sudsing. Allow him to bathe you in his purging love. Lollygagging allowed. Sit, soak, and savor the moment—then enter into a new week squeaky-clean.

Dear Lord, you who understand my unclean thoughts, my scuffed attitudes, and my smudged motives, please cleanse me from all my impurity. I confess that I _____ and I _____. Forgive me for the nasty way I spoke to _____. Liberate me from my degrading habit of _____. Thank you for a clean heart and a fresh start . . . in the sparkling name of Jesus. Amen.

What Time Is It?

There is an appointed time for everything.
And there is a time for every event under heaven.
ECCLESIASTIES 3:1 NASB

Sometimes I feel as though there just isn't enough time for all I want to do. In recent years my interests have diversified (or should I say scattered?). But I realize the sands in my hourglass are sifting at such a pace that I can't possibly chase every whim. I don't have time to become a master gardener, gourmet cook, interior designer, carpenter, pianist, and scholar-extraordinaire. Besides, who would like me if I could do all that?

To do too much is as dangerous as to do nothing at all. Both modes prevent us from savoring our moments. One causes me to rush right past the best of life without recognizing or basking in it, and the other finds me sitting quietly as life rushes past me.

No, I'm not so foolish that I'm going to chase pipe dreams—but rainbows, now that's another story. I know I want to be more than I am today. That means I'll have to use my time wisely, invest myself discerningly, and savor the flavor of every delicious moment assigned to me.

Scripture tells us that there's a right time for everything. Then Solomon lists the times. Let's check in with Sol's "clock" (hear it ticking?) and decide what time it is for us:

a time to give birth (I don't think so.)

a time to die (Hmm, closer.)

a time to plant

a time to uproot (Does this mean I have to move again?)

a time to kill (Huh?)

a time to heal

a time to tear down

a time to build up

a time to weep

a time to laugh (All right!)

a time to mourn

a time to dance (The macarena? Nah.)

a time to throw stones

a time to gather stones (Like diamonds, emeralds, rubies?)

a time to embrace

a time to shun embracing (Hello, teens, are you listening?)

a time to search

a time to give up as lost

a time to keep

a time to throw away (Hey, have you been looking in my closet?)

a time to tear apart

a time to sew together (Uh-oh, I don't do thread.)

a time to be silent (Me?)

a time to speak (Now you're talking.)

a time to love (Smile.)

a time to hate (Shudder.)

a time for war (Sob.)

and a time for peace (Whew.)

That's a lot of savoring. Did you find yourself on Sol's list? What time is it in your life? Perhaps you have a giant problem and it's your time, like the shepherd David, to throw stones. Or maybe you've been mourning the loss of a loved one, a broken dream, or finances, and it's time to step into your dancing slippers. You may be in the midst of a relational fracas, and you know in your heart enough is enough: it's time to mend what has been torn apart. Is there someone you've been shunning with your displeasure? Then for you, it's time to embrace.

Whatever your time, whatever your season, even in the midst of tragedy, there are moments worth savoring. Some of us have more sand on the bottom of our hourglass than on the top. (I'm not referring to our figures, even though they do tend to slip with the sand.) Yet, as long as breath is in our bodies, there will be moments, sweet moments, to revel in. This time is our time. Let's go savor the flavor!

Lord, teach us to enter into the gift of life. Amen.

Snickering

A joyful heart makes a cheerful face.
PROVERBS 15:13 NASB

I was speaking in Colorado Springs in late October, so Les was left at home to give out Halloween treats to any tots who might toddle to our door masquerading as bunny rabbits. That evening he received a dinner invitation too good to pass up, which meant he didn't hand out the bags of goodies he had purchased earlier that day.

I realized we would both look like bloated goats if I didn't get rid of the mountainous candy stash. So one day, as I headed out the door, I filled my pockets with Snickers bars. I had to do some errands in town, and everywhere I went I handed out these miniature candy bars. To friends, to strangers, to salespeople, to women, to children, to men. Without exception they not only were surprised by an unexpected treat, but they all also snickered. Something about the gift caused them to pause, smile, and release a little giggle.

Now, my giving away the candy bars was not what you would call a sacrificial act. But what started initially as a way around my own undisciplined appetite ended up as a reminder for me of how little it takes to brighten a day and a countenance. It was almost as if I had given some people permission for one moment to take a break from the rigors of life and lighten up.

My Mamaw (grandmother) loved peppermint candy. Her somewhat intense personality would brighten if you offered her one. She was not a big eater. In fact, Mamaw would make one plate of food last several days. She was a selective (picky) eater, and not surprisingly she had a lean body frame (some might say bony). But hand her a peppermint, and a smile as wide as her home state of Kentucky would flash across her grateful face.

What does it take to make you unplug from your intensity and giggle? A child's antics? A pet's predicament? A malapropism (now there's a word to bring a smile)? An unexpected note? A rainbow? A bumper sticker?

Barbara is Queen of Bumper Stickers. She has a collection of fun-filled sayings that folks from all over the country have sent to her, and when she shares them in her talks, audiences just hoot. They get the biggest kick out of these quips that succinctly capture some aspect of our lives in unexpected ways. The bumper stickers kind of zing us, and for a giggly moment we get a reprieve from life's crowded highways.

On those highways I have had the privilege of meeting some exceptional people — generous people who give not only store-bought gifts, but also the gift of themselves. For instance, my friend Ginny Lukei is an ingenious gift giver. She loves to surprise people with presents and activities specifically designed with that person in mind. Her gifts are not hastily thrown together to get an obligation over with (I've been guilty of that) but are carefully crafted to bring joy to the recipient.

One gift Ginny has given me many times is her potato rolls. These will make one giggle with delight and jiggle with extra tonnage. You have not fully lived until you have eaten some of these plump, melt-in-your-mouth-and-head-for-your-thighs rolls. Just to think of them causes me to salivate. One time, because it had been so long since we'd seen each other (she lives in California and I live in Michigan), she made a batch of potato rolls and shipped them to me. Only problem was I wasn't home when they arrived, and by the time I returned days later, the rolls were wearing moss-green fur coats. I didn't salivate—more like regurgitate. Green did not become them (or me). More recently I flew to Ginny's and once again indulged myself in her freshly baked potato rolls . . . and I have the thighs to prove it.

Sometimes I delay offering a gift until I can afford just the right thing, when often the right thing is as affordable as a phone call, a card, a song, a poem, a potato roll, or a Snickers. In fact, I think we should declare today Snickers Day from this moment hence. C'mon, girls, load up your purses, briefcases, and tote bags with candy bars for others and let's go on a Snickers toot. Betcha a potato roll that faces will light up, and instead of sighs, for one brief moment you'll hear the joyful sound of giggles.

Lord, I'm so grateful you designed us with the capability to giggle. What a pleasing sound. And what a delightful feeling. Help us to be generous with our giggles and sparse with our frowns. In the pleasing name of Jesus, Amen.

Star Struck

He also made the stars.
GENESIS 1:16

I felt like Michelangelo himself, as I swayed back and forth on my ladder creating a masterpiece. While, I confess, the ceiling I was working on wasn't as lofty as the Sistine Chapel, it was high enough for me, thank you. And I wasn't painting the hand of God; no, it was more like the handiwork of God.

You see, I was pressing the heavenlies into place on my then-young son Jason's bedroom ceiling—luminous stars, hundreds of them, along with planets, and a few comets for flare. One by one I secured them, taking time to scatter some about the perimeter for visual effect. Finally, after the addition of Mars and Pluto, I was done. I then waited for nightfall and the suspenseful unveiling.

When evening overtook our land, I steered Jason, who was blindfolded, up the stairs to his room. (I'm into drama.) Then, *voilà!* I uncovered his eyes, and to my delight (and his longevity), he was pleased. He made all the right sounds. *Oohs* and *aahs* abounded as I pointed to the different parts of the "sky."

I guess I'm like most parents in that I would give my children the world if I could. We feel the sky is the limit for those we love. And isn't it marvelous that we too have a Parent who offers us all that we will ever need? He who hung the sun, the moon, and the stars, surveyed his efforts, and said, (*Voilà!*) "It is good," was pleased to design the universe's wonders and then to present them to us. Imagine that.

I wonder what exclamation escaped Adam when he saw his first rhino, baboon, and ostrich. I bet if he had had a horn, he would have honked it that day. Or think of the series of *oohs* sung by Eve (which was probably the first aria) when she experienced a crimson sunset. And imagine the magnificent view the first couple must have had of the firmament without the distraction and diffusion of city lights and pollution.

Scripture tells us, "Every good and perfect gift is from above, coming down from the Father of the heavenly lights, who does not change like shifting shadows" (James 1:17). Our God is a gift giver. His generosity is obvious in how lavishly he bestows on us rainbows, waterfalls, canyons, and white caps. Few things are as soul-stirring for me as the designs in creation. They cause me to take time out of my busy life to literally brake for joy — visual joy!

As a matter of fact, one day when I was visiting in the desert, a marshmallow cloud formation drizzled over the mountaintop like so much whipped cream. I brought my bike to a standstill and just beheld this delicious scene for thirty-five minutes. Another evening the sunset turned the skyline into a saucer of peaches and cream — absolutely dreamy. The Lord serves up his scrumptious beauty in liberal portions and then invites us to partake. His *voilàs* turn into wonderment for me.

From Marilyn's (Meberg, who else?) patio, she and her guests can view a ring of mountains. I have often joined her at nightfall for the spectacular performance as the sun sets. The mountains go through a series of thrilling changes. From pinks to lavenders to deep purples, the setting sun and emerging evening appear to cover the hillside for sleep. Marilyn and I never tire of the Lord's thrilling displays. We *ooh* and *aah* in all the right places, and we can feel our blood pressure balancing out as smiles and giggles of pleasure help us to express our gratitude. And we, like Adam, would honk if we had a horn.

Lord, in a world so often dark with sin, thank you for the light from your creation that continues to fill our lives with smiles, giggles, gratitude, and hope. Amen.

Pacified

When I was a child . . .
1 CORINTHIANS 13:11

Recently, I had the most mirthful thought; it came to me during church. A man rose during the service and walked up the aisle toward the back carrying his young child. The toddler obviously was not impressed with the sermon. To keep everyone from knowing the extent of the child's displeasure, the father had corked him. A pacifier protruded from the little one's mouth keeping his fussiness firmly bottled. His face appeared a tad red from holding in his opinions, but the pacifier did seem to accomplish its purpose.

Now, here's my thought: I'd like to manufacture adult pacifiers. What do you think? It makes me want to honk and giggle. Too outrageous, you say? Well, not so quick.

Don't you know some pretty fussy people that you'd like to . . . cork? C'mon now, be honest. Why, those rubber stoppers might prevent unnecessary dissension, promote goodwill among humankind, and even breed greater contentment. Are you catching the vision?

I can recall a number of times I should have taken a couple of good swigs on a pacifier instead of a couple of verbal swings at an antagonizer. We would all have been better off if I had. My joy certainly would have increased, for I have found my first words are not always my finest choices. Instead, my reactive whirl of words has the capacity to be outlandish. More often than I'd like to admit, my verbal response is based in an unsteady emotion such as hurt. (And hurt can be as fickle as love.) In my attempt to hide my hurt and protect my vulnerable (and prideful) heart, I have used lashing language that puts others *en garde*. My reaction conveys an inaccurate message. It shouts, "I'm angry" rather than confessing, "I'm hurt."

Also, the sharp edge of lashing language can wound the recipient. In the heat of the moment, that's somewhat satisfying. *Touché!* Yet, when our feelings cool and our brains settle down, we almost always regret our knee-jerk (emphasis on *jerk*) reaction.

That's where the pacifiers fit in. Imagine how differently events would have unfolded if pacifiers had been applied appropriately. For example, picture Peter in the Garden of Gethsemane. Instead of whipping out his sword to whack off the soldier's ear, Peter would have raised his hand indicating a five-minute time-out. Then he'd reach for a small leather sack tied to his waist and pull out a well-worn pacifier. After several reflective pulls on his binkie, he would realize how inappropriate lashing out would be and instead turn to the Lord for direction.

See, this idea has merit. In fact, I can envision these teensy comforters being installed as standard equipment on automobiles. Honk, honk. Then, when the guy on the highway gets in our way, we push a button (instead of laying on the horn) which, in turn, releases our binkie from above our heads. We grab onto our pacifier and, after several deep slurps, feel prepared to continue on our journey more . . . well, pacified.

And what about school? Don't you think every high school should attach binkies to the desks? Then, when belligerence is the 'tude of the moment, teachers and students alike could unwind during a binkie break. Or maybe they could have a binkie room or a pacifier parlor instead of a detention hall. That way the rebellious could ruminate rather than rumble.

I'd manufacture different colored pacifiers to go with our outfits, moods, and decor. I'd give the mouthpieces as gifts, tons of them. I'd offer them personalized, iridescent, flavored, and gold-trimmed. I'd organize pacifier conventions and even have marathons to reward the person who stays plugged the longest.

Only one thing niggles at me about this idea. It's the rest of our opening verse, "I put childish ways behind me." Oh, phooey, that kinda spoils my frivolity.

How about you? Playing any childish games? Need to grow up?

Lord, help me not to look for an easy way out like a child seeking recess or a toddler searching for her pacifier. Help me to take responsibility before you and others for my actions and reactions. Thank you that I can choose to give up my childishness and instead experience childlike joy. Amen.

Treasured Differences

Male and female he created them.
GENESIS 1:27

"Look, honey! Over here, look!" My husband, Les, excitedly called to me. We had been strolling in our hamlet-sized town, window browsing, when he beckoned me. As I approached to see what he had discovered, I noticed he was pointing down at the sidewalk. That's when I stopped in my tracks. There, at his feet, was a dead, squashed mouse.

"Are you crazy or something?" I shot back at him. "Why would I want to see a dead varmint? Have you ever heard me request to see such a disgusting sight? I'm out of here!"

Les lingered over his find as if he hated to leave it. Yikes! Talk about a tilted steering wheel. Men have such a different angle of viewing things than women. We girls call to others to come see a playful puppy, a cuddly kitten, or a cooing baby.

Meanwhile the guys dangle a grass snake like a charm bracelet, point out the newest road kill, and burp loud enough to register 6.3 on the Richter scale.

That's not to say all guys—just a fair portion—go for the yucky stuff of life. But I find the he-men in my vicinity would rather investigate a spider's nest than check out the new lace curtains.

I'm usually grateful that men's angle of viewing is different. But there are times when I agree with the book title that proclaimed, *Men Are from Mars, Women Are from Venus*. Even though we did start out in the same garden, we don't seem to be smelling the same rosebush.

I find it helpful to gain another's perspective; yet at times when I ask my husband for his, I not only don't get his tilt, but we've ended up in some all-out, big-time bouts.

Speaking of bouts, do any of the men in your life watch *Big Time Wrestling?* Talk about Mars—these are planetary goof balls, sportin' crater-sized 'tudes, pouncing on each other while yelling degrading messages. What a sport! No, make that spout. For these are oversized louts who spout and pout.

Actually, my husband is a sport. He frequently goes along with me while I shop for a new outfit and gives me his perspective, which I value because I want him to enjoy how I look. Of course, we don't always concur on clothes. Sometimes we wrestle over selections. (I wish I knew how to do a half nelson.)

We were drawn to each other in the beginning because we didn't agree on many things. Our differences enable us to enlarge each other's angle of viewing life.

Les was from a large family; I was from a small family. His siblings were clustered in age while my brother, sister, and I were spaced a decade or more apart. Needless to say, we related differently in our families. Therefore, we both brought into our marriage our own expectations of family life. It took time and mistakes to come up with an integrated plan that worked for us. Les and I still have a couple of points of contention in our family theology, but we've learned to work around and even through them.

A common, faulty belief holds that true love and romance means harmony of thought. Whereas I'm of the opinion, if we agree on everything, one of us is unnecessary. We have also given up our contribution to the relationship. Besides, I have seen far too many silent partners wake up one day and walk out. To survive without conflict they had moved so far away from their own leanings, interests, beliefs, opinions, and feelings that, when they got back in touch with themselves, they moved away from their mates. The once cooperative mate now doesn't want the static or hard work required to realign the relationship and therefore finds it easier to begin anew with someone who appreciates his or her slant on life.

We need to respect our differing views (not necessarily because the point has merit but because the person does) and to value another's contribution. I will never—hear me on this—never enjoy viewing mushed mice. But I also don't expect Les to get into girl stuff (tea parties, burping Tupperware, sudden bursts of tears).

Lord, thank you that you didn't use a cookie cutter when you designed us. Instead, we are handmade, one of a kind, male and female. May we treasure each other's uniqueness and remember to tilt our steering wheels to see from another angle. Amen.

Friendly Skies

As the heavens are higher than the earth,
so are my ways higher than your ways.
ISAIAH 55:9

I had a 'tude the size of a B52 (a World War II bomber). You see, I wasn't all that thrilled about flying. If the good Lord had meant for us to be up in the air, he would have required us to live in hangars instead of homes.

What prompted my 'tude wasn't just the altitude, the confinement, or the six peanuts they serve as a meal (I give more generous snacks to our family dog). No, it was much more than that.

I can't even say it was the people who board and casually whack off the top of your head with their slung-over-the-shoulder carry-ons as they obliviously bebop down the aisle to locate their seats. (Doesn't bother me, doesn't bother me, doesn't bother me.) Nor do I believe my 'tude inflated simply because of the telephone-booth-size rest rooms that allow you to back in and sidle out. It wasn't even the towel disposal bin, whose location remains a mystery to me.

No, I think my greater gripe was when the 'tude barons boarded. These are the folks who enter the plane with the idea this confined space is theirs to do with as they please. The ones who shove their belongings under your seat, who elbow you repeatedly to expand their comfort, and who talk so loud they can be heard throughout the plane, if not the firmament. Some believe a restricted space with recirculated air is the best place to apply their nail polish or spray a fresh mist of perfume upon their person (never mind the hyperventilating asthmatic next to them).

Yes, all these things gave me a high-flyin' 'tude. Then one day I realized navigating the airways was to be a constant part of my life, and I was going to lose a lot of my joy if I didn't make some altitude adjustments. I needed another perspective.

When I'm willing to view my situations from another angle, often details come into focus I hadn't really thought about before. In fact, once I refocused on my frequent flying, I came up with this list of reasons I'm grateful to be airborne. I'll put on a grati-'tude before boarding because:

1. It provides a way to travel that allows me to dart about the country and do things I could never do otherwise.
2. I've met wonderful people not only after I arrive at my destination but also in the skies (well, most of those people).
3. I can sit down, be still, and maybe even slip in a nap.
4. I have a chance to catch up on some good reading.
5. I have opportunities to be light and salt to an often dark and unseasoned world.
6. I might be able to offer a word of kindness to an anxious traveler or a stressed flight attendant.
7. As unskilled at cooking as I am, I can still offer up a better meal than the airlines.

These are just some of the reasons that caused me to tilt my steering wheel to a different angle so I could see around my attitudes. Now, how about you? Need a new flight plan? Maybe you don't have to take on the friendly skies but instead find yourself taxiing around your home or office with a jet-sized 'tude. Try sitting still (which is hard to do with a revving 'tude) and ask the Lord for a fresh perspective for an old flight pattern or routine. Then prepare for takeoff (bring seat to an upright position, fasten seat belt, stow tray table) and enjoy the amazing view.

Lord, steer me clear of myself long enough that I might gain sight of a higher plan. Amen.

Horsin' Around

His pleasure is not in the strength of the horse, nor his
delight in the legs of a man; the LORD delights in those who
fear him, who put their hope in his unfailing love.
PSALM 147:10–11

Hi-ho, Cecil. Away! No, I didn't mean "Silver." Cecil is my
horse. Well, I don't own her or anything. Actually, I've
only ridden her once but she (or is it he?) is the only horse
with whom I have stayed on speaking terms after a ride.

Here's the scoop (which, gratefully, I didn't have to
use). I had been invited to visit Remuda Ranch, a facility
in Wickenberg, Arizona, dedicated to helping young
women with eating disorders. One of the perks of my
tour was to be a horseback ride. My husband, Les, didn't
think me wise to accept the invitation to ride the dusty
trails. He wasn't worried about the dust, but he was worried about my rust—my rusty horse skills and my rusty
body. And Les wasn't worried about the trail paths so
much as he was my tailbone being splattered on the road-
way. Oh, ye of little faith.

On my arrival Kay, my lovely hostess, greeted me
with enthusiasm. We attended chapel services and then
headed for the stables. My husband's cautions rang in my
ears as I surveyed the saddled horses. I really had
planned to just watch from the sidelines while the others
rode, until I spotted a particular horse.

I thought, *If I did agree to ride, that's the horse I would want*. He reminded me of my childhood days when I watched Roy, Dale, Trigger, and Buttercup on television every week. This horse looked like Trigger, and everyone knows Trigger would only take you on happy trails.

The playful staff encouraged me to ride along. I hesitated until Kay pointed to the horse (alias Trigger) and said he/she would be my steed. That was when I laced up my high-top riding boots and sauntered toward my horse. (Have you ever seen a five-foot person saunter?) The stable staff formally introduced the horse and me.

"Cecil? Cecil!" I repeated, shocked anyone would name Roy's horse Cecil. "Why, Cecil is a sea serpent."

But after they listed Cecil's calm virtues for the tenth time, I gave in and boarded my waiting transportation via a booster box. I assuaged my palpitating heart with the thought that Cecil was only a one-horse-power vehicle.

The six staff members, my daughter-in-law, Danya, and I lined up and headed out. Cecil and I moseyed along pretty well together. In fact, we were makin' tracks. The only challenge I had was my stirrups. They were a little too long for my short legs, and I felt like a toe dancer as I stretched to keep my feet in the stirrups (which had been hiked up as far as they would go).

Soon, as I was jostled to and fro in the saddle, I hit, you might say, my first pothole: My legs began to ache. But I continued on since we had only been riding three minutes. Well, about six minutes into the ride, my leg muscles began to scream, "Are you out of your mind? What do you think you're doing?!" Now my back (my second pothole) began to join in the whining chorus. Evidently my aerobic lifestyle of bench-pressing the newspaper and hoisting the mail had not prepared me for this equine workout.

Finally, with my legs stretched far beyond their designed reach and with a kink in my back the size of New Hampshire, I pleaded my cause with the staff. They immediately and compassionately headed for the stable. As I deboarded Cecil, after an eleven-minute ride, my legs wobbled. I looked like a Weeble as I toddled my way to a bench. For three days afterwards my back felt like Cecil had ridden me.

By the following morning, my wobbling was lessening, but my back continued to make threatening statements. I didn't mention this discomfort to my husband lest he feel, well, right or something.

Do you find it difficult to take good advice? To live within your limitations? To admit when you're wrong? Just remember, if you get a backache from carrying your horse, don't be surprised.

Lord, may we not spend our life-efforts horsing around, but may we gallop toward wisdom. Amen.

Offshoot

> He is like a tree planted by streams of water,
> which yields its fruit in season and whose leaf does
> not wither. Whatever he does prospers.
>
> PSALM 1:3

I brake for trees. Yep, trees. I love all kinds—tall ones, squat ones, full ones, even skimpy ones. I, of course, enjoy trees that produce fruit, flowers, and colorful leaves. I also appreciate tree shade, tree shapes, and tree shadows. I even like tree droppings with the exception of black walnuts, which have an adverse effect on my flowerbeds.

Trees serve as a refuge for climbers, picnickers, tree houses, birds, squirrels, and nuts like me. I find most trees hospitable. In fact, my grandmother had a shade tree so generous it drenched her entire dwelling in soothing shadows, keeping her comfortable throughout the sultry Kentucky summers.

Some of my favorite trees are palm trees. They seem so perky even on their sassy hair (frond) days. That's not easy. When my fronds become unruly so does my 'tude.

The rough patterned bark of the palm interests me. Someone (guess who) spent a great deal of time designing the intricate detailing. When untended, some palms become untidy with dead fronds that look like my morning shredded wheat.

I also am enamored with weeping willows. They are so poetic. On breezy days they become lovely whisk brooms dusting the earth. On summer days their graceful branches lean toward the water's edge drinking in their environment. In a storm they become the eccentric scientist, wild with enthusiasm. And in the winter they take on a melancholy appearance, bowing low with grief.

Yes, yes, I love trees. Trees have inspired many poems. Why, even the village smithy wouldn't have wanted to bang hot iron without the protective covering of the spreading chestnut tree. And someone said he had never seen "a poem as lovely as a tree."

He must have been peering up a redwood. Those will cause one to pull off the road to take a closer gander. Imagine the toothpicks you could produce from one of those branches. I looked like a termite compared to that trunk—an undernourished termite at that. The redwoods cause people to hush and look up in awe. Hmm, maybe that was the idea.

When I was challenged years ago to select a life verse from Scripture, I headed for the trees. I chose Psalm 1:3 and the companion verse in Jeremiah 17:8. The Jeremiah passage compares a bush and a tree. Of course the tree wins. For the tree represents the righteous while the bush is a picture of those who put their trust in people instead of the Lord.

I guess with my five-foot stature I've always felt bushlike, and so my longing has been to grow into a rooted, shooted, fruited tree. (Tall isn't enough; I also want to be productive.) I am especially smitten with the fruit trees that grow in my own yard where I can be the benefactress of the apples and sweet cherries. And that premise carries over into my spiritual life as well. For as much as I love sharing my faith with others, the fruit is even sweeter when it benefits those who live in my own backyard.

What kind of tree are you? Are you planted near the water to avoid disaster should a drought occur? What type of fruit do you bear? Who is benefiting from your fruit?

Lord, thank you for brake-screeching tree sightings that cause us to pull over. It helps us to slow down and admire your creativity. May we purpose to grow up into oaks of righteousness. And may we have the joy of watching our loved ones benefit from our shade and our fruitfulness because of your goodness. Amen.

Z-Z-Z

And how delightful is a timely word!
PROVERBS 15:23 NASB

Whatkind of a communicator are you? Are you a babbling brook, a quiet stream, or a thunderous waterfall? Do you have volumes of verbiage like the *Encyclopedia Britannica?* Or are you a selective and simple speaker like a Dick and Jane primer? Most folks probably fall somewhere in between.

I'm more a whirlwind of words; I know that surprises you. Don't you wonder how a five-foot woman could have a ten-foot capacity for verbosity? Just lucky, I guess. Although some may take issue . . . like my friend Lana.

Lana and I have been cohorts for years. We have had miles of smiles. We have traveled together, spoken at conferences together, spent holidays together, and played endless games of Scrabble. We laugh, squabble, commiserate, dream, debate, and converse.

Boy, can we converse! Well, okay, maybe I do tend to have a few more words to express than she does, but then, who's counting? Surely not me. I don't do numbers, just words. Actually, Lana can hold her own once she gets started. But my bursts of babble have been known to wear her down and out before she can begin.

I remember . . . Lana and I had just completed an exciting but exhausting seminar. We were sharing a room, and I was wound tighter than a tick from days of working with fascinating people. My way to debrief was to release my thoughts in squalls, blustery reports of days of details. I'm usually aware when I'm, say, too much for my listeners, but evidently this time I lost track of my mouth-monitor.

It wasn't that I had bored Lana into a mild stupor. No, evidently I had knocked her plumb out. I realized this when I hovered over her reclining frame to emphasize some critical point in my narrative. She was no longer conscious. Z's slipped effortlessly through her exhausted lips, and her eyelids were sealed like Ziploc baggies, suggesting our talk had been terminated. How rude! And I was just getting to the good part.

Since then Lana and I have chortled over that abbreviated conversation many times. She claims she had heard enough. I, on the other hand, know I had more to say . . . much, much more.

While some folks may need to cut back on fat grams, shopping sprees, and/or television viewing (okay, I do too), a slew of us need to reduce our rambling recitals. Silence is not empty but, in fact, often fuller than our many words. So instead of trying to fill every quiet moment with chatter, we would do well to sit ever so still (shh) and develop a new skill: listening. In doing so we might hear the Z's of a companion attempting to get a well-deserved break. Or perhaps we would hear the Lord speaking ever so softly to us.

Lord, please speak loud enough for us to hear you over our clamoring hearts. For some of us, even when we're not talking, we still have a lot of noise going on inside. We are amazed, Lord, that you never tire of hearing us talk to you. That's quite an extravagant truth — for no one has ever cared for us like that till you. Amen.

Ticked

The wise heart will know the proper time.
ECCLESIASTES 8:5

Remember the Tidy Bowl Man? Well, I think his brother lives in my clock! Honest, someone is in my clock trying to get out. I can hear him tapping. If I knew Morse code, maybe I could decipher his little pleas for help. Day and night, more on than off, tap, tap, tap. Since it's a clock radio, maybe the tapping is actually the Tidy Bowl Brother (T.B.B.) dancing. Maybe his taps are raps. Perhaps this is Radio Rapper. Then again, T.B.B. may just be fed up with being trapped by time and wants someone to heed his frustration.

We all seem to live by the ever-tapping clock. Frequently, when I ask a friend to join me for tea, I hear, "I wish I could, but I have to make it to _____." Fill in the blank with "my appointment," "my plane," "my deadline." We huff and puff through our hours wondering where, oh where, the day has gone. Perplexing, isn't it, how little and at times how much can be accomplished with the moments we've been given?

I'm usually running behind, playing catch up, and robbing Petula to pay Paulette. Yet give me a day off, and it slips through my fingers (like my last paycheck). Then, the harder I try to hang on to special moments, the faster the clock seems to tick. Which ticks me off because the hard days, the painful days, the boring days, seem to contain endless hours.

All told, at the age of fifty-two, my years have been as the Scripture said they would be, "like a vapor." Poof! Fifty-two years have come and gone.

At the close of a day, I always mentally run back through my accomplishments or lack thereof. The thereofs are the aggravating tap, tap, tapping reminders and rap, rap, rapping regrets about what I didn't do or should have done. You know what? I think the Tidy Bowl Brother and I might be kindred spirits. I too feel encased within a timepiece that can at times rob me of my peace. Instead of tapping or rapping, my way of dealing with the ever-present clock is flapping. I spread my stubby wings and try to lift my chubby frame off the ticking tarmac only to crash-land like one of those gooney birds who flails beak-first into the earth.

Earth is the problem, you know. As long as we remain bound to the earth in this life, we will be restricted by an ever-present ticking-tapping clock. When the day comes that we are freed from time and enter our sweet liberty, we will never again have to consult a Big Ben or a Bulova. Hallelujah! Until then, we need to make peace with the timepiece so we, unlike the T.B.B., don't spend our time beating our heads against the clock. Here are some tips. I'll try them if you will.

1. Don't cram every day so full you can't enjoy the journey.
2. Don't underplan and miss the thrill of a fruitful day.
3. Don't underestimate a nap, a rocking chair, and a good book
4. Don't become a sloth.

5. Do offer your gratitude for the moments assigned to you.
6. Do celebrate even the passing of days. (For he designed it thus—poof!)
7. Do enter into your time here on earth not flapping but soaring. Ride out your days with a sense of your limitless future in a timeless eternity.

Lord, thank you for the structure of time so we don't flit or flap away our days. Help us to rest and to run in right proportions. For left unto ourselves, some of us would race and others of us would rust. Either way we would speed past or sleep through the joy. Teach us, Lord, to value our days and redeem our moments. In Jesus' everlasting name. Amen.

Barking Up the Wrong Me

Look upon my affliction and rescue me.
PSALM 119:153 NASB

I have been doing the most ridiculous thing, and trust me it has not added one iota to my joy. I am baby-sitting. No, not for a chubby-cheeked, cooing cherub. I only wish that were the case. I am tending to a dog. No, not one that bounds about the house with frisky enthusiasm, for that actually would tickle me. It's not even an old pooch who agreeably curls up in the corner and snores. I'd probably join him. I could even deal with a snarling, chew-off-the-sofa-leg kind of mutt compared to this one.

Instead, my tend-ee is a virtual pet. Yep, you read it right. I'm jumping through cyberspace hoops, so to speak, trying to care for this unnamed, unclaimed, onscreen mongrel.

It all started when I saw these futuristic playmates dangling harmlessly from a wall in a small shop in my hometown. These items are pocketsize and conveniently attached to key chains.

We were going to visit our nephew Joshua, and I thought this would make a great gift for him. That was before I activated the computer-prompted pup.

On the long drive to Joshua's (540 miles), I decided I would figure out how this pet operated so I could teach Josh. I opened the package, started the action, then leaned back to read the fine print. Well, 350 miles later I was still trying to understand the directions. (The manufacturer's tape that partially covered the instructions didn't help. But I'm not sure I would have understood even if all the info were available to me.)

Because I didn't "get it," the dad-blamed gadget kept beeping at me. I understood enough to realize when it beeped it was signaling me to do something for this animated animal. But what, pray tell, was I to do?

I learned along our travels that once activated I was responsible for this dog's longevity (talk about a load). This meant if I didn't tend to it in a timely and correct manner, the pup would leave home and cease to exist. Talk about a guilt trip.

The first night before reaching our destination, Les and I stayed at a motel. All evening the little handheld machine tweeted repeatedly, summoning me. At first its little pleas for help fed my codependent heart, and I merrily tried to figure out which buttons to push to care for its needs. But, as the evening wore on, my nerves wore thin with the insistent shrill beeping. Even irritated, though, I continued to care for my charge, thinking I'd soon hand him over to Josh. Talk about a misconception.

By the time we arrived the following day, I realized this pet was too complex for young Joshua. Well, then I'd just have to find someone older to give it to, I assured myself. Think again. No one wanted, needed, or desired the pipsqueak.

For days I walked around with this neurotic aggravation tucked in my pocket, making demands on my life.

Have you ever seen one of these pesky pets? If not, listen up. You have to feed the pup, bathe him, give him shots, discipline him, play catch with him, put him to bed, and clean up his smelly deposits. C'mon, that's more than I'm willing to do for my husband. If that's not enough, this mutt-machine has a report card that grades how well you're doing and how pleased your pet is with your behavior.

That was the final straw. A report card, why, that's ludicrous. If you think I'm lugging this yapping thing through life then think again!

Think? Hmm, think.

Perhaps that's what I should have done to begin with— put a little more purchasing thought into my decision.

Have you made any hasty decisions lately? Are they causing you unnecessary pressure? What can you do about it? What kind of a decision-making report card would you give yourself?

Lord, how often do we lose our joy over something we got ourselves into? Thank you that you do rescue us and that you grade us mercifully. Amen.

Say "Cheese"

See, I have engraved you on the palms of my hands.
ISAIAH 49:16

Picture this: years of photographic debris littered hither and yon; some photos crammed in drawers, taped on mirrors, stacked on desks, magnetized to the refrigerator, stuffed in shoe boxes, propped against window frames, crinkled up in purses, pressed in old books, mixed in with the bills.... This is indicative of how for years I have handled our family's pictorial history.

I've always meant to organize, alphabetize, and categorize these frames of life, but I'm not naturally organizational, alphabetical, or categorical. In fact, I'm more eclectic in my approach to life. Some might say I'm a willy-nilly, helter-skelter, or if-you-can-find-it-you-can-have-it kind of person. Now, don't get me wrong; I like a tidy environment. Just don't open a door or drawer without taking some precautions. That is, if you can yank them open and then force them closed again. But if you do pry open a drawer, would you mind seeing if you could find the three rolls of film I misplaced from our family vacation, summer 1992? I know they are here somewhere.

I also know I need to get a grip on our photos. So I took the following action. First, I conducted a pictorial roundup. All floaters were brought into the living room and put inside Les's grandfather's trunk that presides in front of our couch. This activity actually took weeks, as we rooted around retrieving wayward pictures from strange and unusual locations (medicine cabinet, toolbox, clothes dryer).

Once the majority had been packed into the trunk, I purchased albums of all sizes. Then I sat down in front of the mountainous heap, and in a brief time became overwhelmed with this wide-load project. I couldn't figure out how to separate them into categories. Should it be by years, events, houses, individuals, vacations, celebrations, crises, or all of the above?

Actually, I couldn't even figure out who some of these folks were. I mean, who in the world let these strangers into our house? Like the guy with the cigar and the big schnozzola. Where did he come from? Or the woman in the tattered flapper dress swinging a hula hoop around her doughy midsection? (Oops, never mind; that's me in my nightgown.) And who are all these babies? Portly babies, pining babies, puckered babies, peaceful babies. Why, I could start a pediatrics ward — or an orphanage, since their names remain a mystery.

This brings me to my next dilemma: How does one toss out a picture without guilt? A person's likeness is so personal it seems like a violation to discard them. After all, what if these individuals have rejection issues?

Les and I were in an antique shop the other day when we spotted a photo album on a table. Interested, we peeked inside only to find a family peering back at us.

We both felt sad seeing someone's snapshots cast aside for strangers to peruse. We wondered who would throw away his or her history (a few family members maybe, but the whole clan)? And who would purpose to buy more relatives?

Gradually, I'm making progress with the development of our albums and have in courageous moments thrown out a few strangers (not the cigar man; I've bonded with him). I've even parted with a myriad of duplicates. (I had forty-seven outside shots of one of our homes. Perhaps my finger stuck, or the camera was new, or my hot flashes and the camera flashes were in competition — who knows? I've thinned them down to twenty-nine.)

My eighty-three-year-old mom recently condensed her life, and guess what she gave me — a chestful of unidentified photographs. Yikes! Back to searching for identity clues.

Ever feel like your identity is lost in a world full of people? We have a God whose heart is expansive enough to hold us all and yet who's so intently focused on each of us that he knows our rising up and our sitting down.

Meditate on Psalm 139. Then smile pretty; heaven's watching.

-ò-

Dear Lord, thank you that you are a God of order and that you never lose track of us. We are comforted to know that once we're in your family we will never be discarded. It fills us with joy realizing you have framed us with your love and view us through your mercy. Our faces are no surprise to you, Lord, and our identities are engraved in the palms of your hands. (Whew.) Amen.

Brand Spanking New

Put on the new self.
EPHESIANS 4:24

When I stopped by my friends Gene and Ruthann Bell's home, I had no idea a miracle had just occurred on their premises. Ruthann proudly led me down their wooded lane and through the barn. Then she opened the large wooden door into the back barnyard. There, standing next to his stately mother, Mariah (a registered Morgan), was a wee colt.

Christened Huw (Welsh spelling for "Hugh" and named for the character Huw Morgan in *How Green Was My Valley,* a Welsh novel), the five-hour-old newborn teetered and tottered on his spindly legs. He eyed us with caution as he leaned in closer to his mom. Then, when Mariah moved into the open corral, the colt tried to scamper after her. His knobby legs kept tangling up on him. We laughed the kind of sweet laughter that comes from taking delight in the wonders of new life.

What pleasure I found in observing this bony bundle toddling, testing his unpolished prance, trying out his touchy brakes while never straying far from his mother. The colt instinctively knew to nuzzle in to her for nourishment, comfort, and protection.

Ever wish you could start over? Probably all of us have longed for another chance in some area of our lives. We wouldn't necessarily have done things differently, just more or perhaps less. For starters I wish I would have read more when I was in school (when I could still retain), and I wish I had griped less when I was a young mom.

The truth is we can't go back, only forward into uncharted territory. To sit in our sorrow would lead to misery. Although regret that leads to change is a dear friend, regret that leads to shame is a treacherous enemy.

So how do we live without allowing regret to rob us of our joy? How about this insight to prompt us on: "And lean not on your own understanding" (Prov. 3:5).

Sometimes we are so certain we know something, when, dear sisters, we don't really. Know what I mean? There is no guarantee that if we had done a part of our lives differently things would end up any different. We have to trust the God of the universe who directs the outcome of all things that he will do that which ultimately needs to be done (in spite of us, if necessary).

I'm not suggesting we don't need to take responsibility for past mistakes or that we shouldn't learn to do things more honorably, for these are changes that lead to fresh beginnings. But I am saying many things are now out of our control but never his.

So next time you and I need something to lean on, let's make it the Lord. Then we can nuzzle in and receive what we need most—nourishment from his Word, comfort from his Spirit, and the protection of his presence.

Leaning in also offers us the benefit of no regrets and an opportunity to "put on the new self."

Lord, thank you that as we lean into you for nourish-ment, comfort, and protection (fill 'er up), we then can enter into our fresh beginnings (new day, job, resolve) with enthusiasm. May it delight you, Lord, to see us toddle and sometimes prance in our efforts, and may it even cause you to throw back your head and laugh with sweet abandon. Amen.

Prompted

It is good to praise the LORD and make music to your name,
O Most High, to proclaim your love in the morning
and your faithfulness at night. . . . For you make me glad
by your deeds, O LORD; I sing for joy at the works
of your hands. How great are your works, O LORD,
how profound are your thoughts!
PSALM 92:1–2, 4–5

I can remember the days when I bounded from bed in the morning, motor revving, ready to face the world. Well, okay, maybe I never truly bounded in the morning, but I know I had more days in which I hit the highway hollerin' than I have now. Today sludge moves faster than I do.

And moan . . . oh, my, you should hear the series of groans that escape my lips as I force my frame into an upright position. The first couple of steps I attempt, boy, are they doozies, full of verbal rumblings. My body's soundtrack combines the creaks of an ancient door with the travailing of a birthing basset hound. Somehow, making these painful proclamations to express my physical struggle helps me trudge forward. I'm like an unoiled machine, an unprimed pump, and an unchained melody (that means I'm four notes short of a tune). I definitely need daybreak prompting.

I must admit the mirror is not the prompting monitor I had in mind. By the time I drag my weary body to the bathroom to face my reflection, it is a tad off-putting, to say the least. Though my bed-head does add humor, doesn't yours? Hair skittering in all directions with occasional wads spewing up like oil wells and knotted clumps secured to the scalp. It makes one wonder what one must have been dreaming about to cause such turbulence.

Here's the good news. We can only get better looking now that we're up. A good brushing, curling, back combing, spraying, and our hair begins to make sense — like it's supposed to be attached to our heads. Once we've adorned our frames with fashions, shod our feet with footwear, and covered our . . . our . . . our crevices with makeup, we are ready for a new day.

Actually, I need this rigorous (yes, for me this is rigorous) morning regimen to thoroughly wake me up. It shakes out the kinks in my body, dislodges the corrosion from my brain cells, and reactivates my lethargic will . . . kinda.

Imagine, Lord, that we would be reluctant to enter into a new day that you have carefully designed. Forgive our lagging bodies for not skipping in anticipation of your profound plans. Even when our bones lack their original suppleness, may our spirits be flexible so we can joyously stretch to meet with you. Our bodies may be slowing; yet, Lord, may our interior world be growing.

We are grateful our good looks are not dependent on our disintegrating appearance. Lasting beauty emanates from you, Christ. You are our inner loveliness.

For your beauty spills out a covering of grace allowing even the weariest, eldest, and crinkliest of your children (like me) to look her best.

May your Holy Spirit be our daily prompter, and may we be your pleasing responders. May our wretched morning rumblings and grumblings turn to peals of praises and prayers. Amen.

Missing in Action

My people have been lost sheep.
JEREMIAH 50:6

Do you know what I'm tired of? Of course you don't, but I asked that so I could tell you. I have to tell someone, because it's pressing down on my threadbare nerves. I'm tired of looking for things. There, I said it. I spend a great deal of energy—mental and physical—looking for lost, misplaced, and hidden stuff. I find the hunt frustrating, even maddening, and frequently unnecessary.

Take my glasses. You might as well; someone does every time I set them down. I often have to solicit my family's help in searching the premises for my bifocals. My family thinks I should hire my own posse because of the frequency with which I need help rounding up my belongings. I'm afraid they're right.

Keys, purse, and vital papers elude me. I know they can't walk off, but I have wondered if the Tidy Bowl Brother who constantly taps inside my clock has something to do with my ongoing dilemma. Maybe he has a trap door, and he and his brother rifle through my belongings and then scurry off to hide my stuff. All right, all right. I know it's my absentminded personality, not the Tidy Bowl Brother.

Here's what I think would help me and others prone to lostness—Velcro. More specifically, Velcro bodies. Think about it. Instead of laying down my glasses, I'd just press them on the outside of my upper arm. Then, when I needed them, I'd have them. The same with my keys. I could press my car key on one ear lobe and the house key on the other. Practical, handy, and within an arm's reach at any given moment.

Of course, the Velcro thing could get tricky when people shook hands or, worse yet, hugged. Getting shed of the other person might be touchy if not painful. And what if we Velcroed our glasses onto someone else without realizing it?

Oh, never mind. Back to the drawing board.

Velcro couldn't help me with my directions anyway. First off, I lose numbers. They just slip through my brain like money through my fingers. Second, I don't have a working grip on north, south, east, and west. And third, I'm a tad off center, and when under pressure, I can't remember my right from my left. Now, on a calm day, that's not a problem. But when I'm searching for, say, a specific street and traffic is heavy, I've been known to turn into one-way traffic—all headed toward me!

Nothing is worse than not knowing where you are. I remember flying into an airport in southern California and waiting for someone to pick me up. No one came. To make matters worse, I didn't know the names of the people who were supposed to tend to me. After an extended wait, the Skycaps took note of my ongoing presence and became concerned. They even stopped anyone who drove slowly past the outdoor luggage retrieval and asked them if they were looking for me. How embarrassing.

It turned out my driver was at another airport waiting for me. The Skycaps were flipping coins to see who would adopt me, when finally I was paged. My driver, relieved to find me, said she would be there as soon as she could. So, after another hour, when she pulled up, the Skycaps cheered her arrival. They ran my luggage to her car and wouldn't accept a tip. Their lost lamb had found her shepherdess.

Gratefully we do have a Shepherd—and he's not waiting at the wrong airport. He is the Good Shepherd who will seek out the stray lambs and bring them back to the safety of the fold. He promises he will never leave us nor forsake us. He is one who sticks closer than a brother (or Velcro).

Thank you, Lord, for understanding the extent of our lostness—and for never tiring of finding us. Amen.

Flighty

Flowers appear on the earth; the season of singing has
come, the cooing of doves is heard in our land.
SONG OF SONGS 2:12

You've heard of right-brained and left-brained. Well, I'm
bird-brained. No, not in regard to my cranial capacity
but referring to my love for winged creatures. A portion of
my brain takes great delight in the flight and fancy of birds.

I don't love all birds equally. For instance, I'm not ter-
ribly fond of vultures or dodo birds. Now the gooney bird,
he's pretty entertaining, and the turkey, though not
exactly handsome, does trigger some succulent memories of holiday fare.

Even though I'm a bird-brained gal, I don't own any —
birds that is. Unless we were to count the darting hum-
mingbirds who entertain Les and me daily with their aer-
ial bouts outside our home. Like shimmering, streaked
commas they hover over blossoms, sipping sweet nectar.
Or the black-capped chickadees who show up in their
dapper attire and sing among the apple blossoms. And
the cardinals flash their red brilliance as they dart
between the blue spruce. I'd like to think they are all
mine. I mean, I do feed them and at times clean up after
them. Hmm, sorta like family.

My all-time favorite feathered friend would have to be
the bluebird. Perhaps because seeing one is such an occa-

sional happening it's a thrill when suddenly this blue wonder crosses your path. Besides, if you ever see the sunlight refract off their feathers, your heart will take flight. The blue in bluebird takes on new meaning as you memorize their unduplicated color. Amidst this sea of blue feathers is a blush of orange on their breast.

Bluebirds love open fields and fence posts. They aren't seed eaters; so to draw them into country yards takes birdhouses (mounted on fence posts) and birdbaths. We erected those items with wonderful success when we lived outside of town. Since we're once again city slickers, we no longer have the delight of daily visits. Now I have to be satisfied with glass bluebirds in my windowsills and antique bluebird dishes. But when I close my eyes and reminisce, I can still see them luxuriating in our birdbath, pleasing me beyond measure.

Have you noticed the mention of birds in the Scriptures? The Psalms say, "How lovely are Thy dwelling places, O LORD of hosts! The bird also has found a house, and the swallow a nest for herself, where she may lay her young" (Ps. 84:1, 3 NASB).

I choose to believe the "bird" is referring to a bluebird. Besides, the swallows and the bluebirds, even though they compete with each other for housing, are usually in nesting proximity. In this verse both birds have found lovely dwelling places. I like that. In fact, it mentions the birds even nest on the Lord's altars and how blessed are those who dwell in the house of the Lord. Hmm, even the birds can be examples.

David prayed for "the wings of a dove" that he might fly far away from his problems and be at rest (Ps. 55:6). I can get into that, can't you? At times I just want a fast, easy way out. I want to make my way to a hammock strung between two oaks at the water's edge where choirs of songbirds sing me to sleep.

Matthew tells us, "Look at the birds of the air; they do not sow or reap or store away in barns, and yet your heavenly Father feeds them. Are you not much more valuable than they?" (Matt. 6:26). Our heavenly Father provides for the birds. What a lovely thought; he too is a bird-watcher. And to think his care and provision for us is even greater, for he is a people-watcher as well. How comforting.

Father, thank you that you use all you have created to speak to us of your love . . . even the birds. Amen.

What a Pain

Your rod and your staff, they comfort me.
PSALM 23:4

On a peppy morning, thinking myself more athletic than I was or ever will be, I barreled down our second-floor stairwell and missed a step. My feet went skyward, and my tailbone came crashing down onto the exceedingly solid earth. Yikes! I hit a note so piercing neighborhood dogs had to be rushed in to the vet for treatment. Boy, did that smart. Well, smart might be too generous of a word for the situation.

Later I waddled back to the stairwell and counted the steps; they were all there. How I missed one I have no idea—although I have never been good at math. I did note, however, it was a long spell before I forgot that acrobatic equation. The touchy nature of the injury—or at least its tender location—meant pain every time I sat down.

Pain can be such a pain. I hate hurting; it's so draining. Besides, it can restrict our lifestyle, limit our activities, and dishearten us. It's hard to, say, play musical chairs with any enthusiasm when your tailbone is throbbing to the tune of *The Old Gray Mare.* Yet I have learned pain has purpose, which, at the peak of excruciating discomfort, brings me little consolation. Hindsight, though, has often proven pain's value. In fact, I have found pain to be one of life's most effective teachers. It gains one's full attention. It takes lessons down to the bottom (no pun intended) line (step).

A world without pain sounds great. But would it be?

My husband, Les, was returning from a restaurant/ grocery store run. He had diet Pepsi in one hand and Chinese takeout in the other. His shoes were covered in snow as he stepped onto our tiled floor. That's where a calamity occurred that would change our lives. Les's feet went heavenward, and his body headed for that exceedingly solid earth. When his body landed, it was wedged between two walls. The angle and impact left his right ankle with four fractures.

Our son Marty and friend Dan helped me to escort Les to the emergency room. When the doctor asked Les what had happened, he told her I pushed him down the stairs while he was holding his six-pack. Thank you, Les. I assured her that I hadn't pushed him, there were no steps, and that the six-pack was pop. I was pleased to see his offbeat humor was still intact. But we were unaware of what this break meant for Les, or we might not have been chuckling. I did note the doctor's somber demeanor but wrote it off to one too many patients.

After Les spent months in a cast, we thought the tough part was over. But Les's diabetes added complications. When his cast was removed, we thought he was free to resume a walking lifestyle, which he did. His ankle was three times its normal size, but he had no pain. We continued on with life's daily demands. After a number of weeks, I noticed the side of his foot looked unnatural. We visited the doctor and found out that Les's ankle couldn't support his weight. It had begun to disintegrate, and the side of his foot, between his ankle and his heel, had caved in.

Les has been in a newfangled walking cast now for six months; the doctors are predicting he will have to wear it for years to come. At this stage he can only be on his feet ten minutes each hour. Life for us, in the time it took to slip, has changed.

Les didn't realize damage was occurring to his ankle because he had no pain. Had he felt the disintegration, he would have gone for medical counsel before such irreversible damage had occurred. Pain can save our lives both physically and spiritually. Pain alerts us to problems. Pain assists in setting healthy boundaries. Pain can guide us into necessary changes.

The next time you feel pain—emotional or physical— remember that hurt can guide you to live more wisely and within the limits God has chosen to set for you individually. Ask him for insight into what adjustments you should make spiritually, physically, and emotionally to live within those limits. And then ask for the grace to do so.

Dear Lord, we are comforted to realize you can use even pain for our benefit. Amen.

Championship Play

The tongue of the wise makes knowledge acceptable.
PROVERBS 15:2 NASB

I would like to introduce you to my friend Maven, whom, by the way, I happen to hate. I know, I know, we shouldn't hate—and if we do, we surely shouldn't publish the fact. But Maven isn't exactly real, although he does have a consistent personality—aggravating. The reason I say he is my friend is because I have purposed to spend time in his company, and we converse regularly. Maven is a man of extensive vocabulary, and trust me, he has an immovable will.

You see, Maven is my computer Scrabble opponent. He came built into my favorite word game so I would always have someone to challenge, but he doesn't play fair. In fact, he often speaks a language I don't understand—and without apology. Our game-playing relationship has developed by degrees. We started out as novices and have made our way to championship bouts. I don't mind when Maven wins . . . well, perhaps I do, but I wouldn't if he would communicate more clearly. C'mon, listen in and see what you think.

I scan my tiles and decide on the word *boast* to begin the game. Maven, who continually boasts, attaches to *boast* the word *teleosts*. Okay, troops, what is *teleosts*? I stop the game and look it up. It is a bony fish (and Maven is a bonehead).

Next I spell the word *brains*, which I'm obviously in need of. It connects to a double-word score. Things are looking up. My opponent puts down *eme. Eme? Eme?*

"Maven, you're pushing me." I look up *eme*, and I'm told it means "an uncle." Hmm, I'm beginning to suspect a conspiracy between Maven and the built-in Scrabble dictionary, which was probably written by Maven's Uncle Eme.

I then arrange my tiles to spell *elite*. So there, Mav.

He takes his turn and spells out *enure*. I look it up and am told it means "inure." Oh, that really clears things up. So I challenge *inure* and find out it means, "to accept something unacceptable."

"Maven, you're unacceptable!" I yell.

I toss down the word *pilot*. Maven adds to the board *ratton*. Yikes! This guy really gets on my nerves. So I head for the dictionary again. *Ratton* means "rat." Hmm, fitting.

I exchange five of my letters to improve my rack. Maven pauses. (Did I hear someone chortle?) Then he empties his entire rack to create the word *coopting*, with the "g" landing on the triple-word score. *Coopting*, I discover, means to "elect," and so I elect to quit!

A graphic in the electronic Scrabble game as you depart the system depicts the game board being thrown down and shattering into a gazillion pieces. I like that a lot. It feels extremely satisfying; almost as if I got in the last word.

Words can open our understanding, but words can also bring us into conflict with others. At times it's as if our opponents (husband, child, friend, stranger) have been speaking an unknown language. For we haven't understood them nor have they had a clue as to what we were trying to convey.

We need to take the time to search out each other's meanings and not treat our relationships like a game in which we rack up points. Let's not quit trying, let's not throw in the towel, and let's not walk away angry (although breaks can be helpful). Perhaps then we can hear beyond the words to the language of the heart.

You, Lord, are our champion. Teach us to value people even more than the tantalizing last word. May we lean in and truly hear each other. Amen.

Lastly

So the last will be first, and the first will be last.
MATTHEW 20:16

Something about a last word is tasty. It's like the maraschino cherry sitting atop a hot fudge sundae—a pleasing, final touch. But, like the cherry, we often could have done without it.

The dictionary says *last* means "final." Whenever I pulled my mom's rubber-band emotions taut, she would threaten, "This is the last time I'm going to tell you." I usually could weigh by the tone of her voice if she meant really last or just close to last. Sometimes I called it right and sometimes . . . well, let's just say she left a final impression.

Then there's the last straw. "Okay, I've had it! That was the last straw!" We pitchfork this barnyard threat toward others to let them know their pigs have swilled in our mud for the last time, and we're calling in Oscar Mayer.

And what about the last laugh? Doesn't that have a rather odious sound? It makes a person want to hire rear guards to protect oneself from the stinging guffaws of a spiteful comedian. The last laugh sounds like a concoction of revenge with a twist of sardonic humor. Funny? Probably not, and lethal to swallow.

The last hurrah speaks of another final moment. Now, that one makes me feel melancholy. It's as if we're suggesting not only that the party is over, but also that we'll never be invited to another. Then again, it could mean we're about to leave something truly memorable, and we're adding an exclamation point to the festivities. Hurrah! I like that.

The last minute is how I live most of my life. I tend to downshift when I should be accelerating and vice versa. This on-the-edge habit leaves me breathless, frustrated, and a little ditzy (and a little can go a long way). For some reason, in those last minutes, reality thumps me upside the head, and life finally comes into focus, which leaves me scurrying to catch up.

An important last for me is last names. I love my last name, Clairmont. I think it's so French, so romantic. My maiden name was McEuen. Good, strong name but not very, uh, poetic. In high school my best friend was Carol McEachern. When we would meet new folks, and they would ask us our names, our response caused laughter. We were accused of having made up our names. Trust me, if we had, we would have created far more Hollywood-ish or fairy tale-ish ones. On second thought, had we not had those names, we might never have become school chums (we sat in class alphabetically), and then we would never have enjoyed forty years of invaluable friendship.

How about the last dance? When Les and I were young, we promised to save that for each other. Our commitment still stands thirty-six years later.

"Last leg" is a phrase you hear every now and then. It suggests having used up all the other options, which is a sad state to be in, and one I hope to avoid.

Then there's the Last Supper, which for our Lord was tinged with sadness as he tried to prepare himself and his disciples for the ordeal before them. But the Last Supper has become the Lord's Supper for us, and while it reminds us of our sorrowful, sinful state, it also causes us to recall he who gave us reason to celebrate.

Some say we are living in the last days. I'm not prophetic, but I'm also not blind. Many scriptural signs point to our living in the closing chapter of history. But since the Lord's timing and ours are often so different, I'm not holding my breath. In fact, my heart's longing is that my last breath (whether at his coming or my leaving) be one of praise to him who gave his life and who gave me life.

If you could choose what your last will (carefully chosen act) and testament (words that testify to the heart of your life) would be, what would you pick?

Jesus, you are the first and the last. You are the Alpha and Omega. You spell out meaning for our existence. And you are the One who will have the last word. Come quickly, Lord Jesus. Amen.

I See . . . Sorta

The lamp of the body is the eye.
MATTHEW 6:22 NASB

The last time I ordered new glasses I had no-glare coating put on the lenses. That way, when I'm on a platform speaking, I don't refract light like some kind of Star Wars invader every time I turn my head. That no-glare stuff really works great, but as in most enhancements, there is a side effect—my lenses smudge easily. In fact, I'm constantly viewing life through thumbprints, which eliminates a lot of life's little details like steps, curbs, and hedges.

Besides the threat of being tripped up, I have to crinkle my face to see through the fog (like I need another crop of deep-set lines in my face). But I think the most disturbing aspect of this smudge factor is that everyone else notices my lenses are a smeared mess. It's sort of like the junk I hide under my bed. I know it's there, but I don't want anyone else to view it. People even offer to clean my glasses for me. How embarrassing. Actually, their efforts only seem to rearrange the design of the smudges. The last set looked similar to the streaming-star effect of going to hyper speed on Han Solo's Millennium Falcon. I'm constantly asked, "How do you see through them?" Well, I don't know. I guess I've adjusted to people looking like walking trees.

Tonight I walked into an optometry store and asked the attendants to remove the no-glare treatment. They looked at me as if I had said, "My name is Chewbacca."

The first gal shot a glance at the other and said, "Is it possible to reverse this process?"

The other one shrugged her shoulders, pleading ignorance as she headed toward me. Staring at the glasses perched atop my nose, she quipped, "How do you see through those?" Here we go again. "Let me clean them for you," she offered. I could see that one coming.

Meanwhile, her cohort had chatted with the specialist in the back who said he could only do the reversal if I had bought the glasses from their store, which I hadn't. Out of frustration, the girl handed back my glasses, telling me they wouldn't come clean (surprise, surprise). She recommended I invest in new lenses, which (surprise, surprise) they could do for me for a little less than a Princess Leia face-lift.

I left in my usual fog, promising to return if I could see my way clear to buy new spectacles. Then I stumbled through the mall wondering how life would look if I stepped out from behind my cumulus clouds.

There are some advantages in not seeing clearly, you know. I mean, even the little I can see clearly in the morning mirror hasn't been all that wonderful. To see clearly could be more of a reality check than I'm ready for. If my house truly came into focus, I might have to do something radical—like vacuum. Not to mention the obligation I'd feel to weed the garden, wash the windows, and polish the silver. Nah, on second thought, who needs new glasses?

Hmm, I believe blessed fog may be a fairly common approach to life (like a cold). For instance, have you ever paced wide circles around a scale lest you step on the thing and see your Social Security number pop up? Or have you ignored a health issue lest the doctors install R2D2 parts in your anatomy? Or maybe you've been tiptoeing around an issue between you and someone else, hoping it would vaporize while, in reality, it grows more complex with each passing day.

Jesus, forgive us when we resist looking honestly at our lives. For unwillingness to face the truth will lead us far from you. Give us the courage to press into reality. We don't want to live in denial. Denial has to do with darkness and you, dear Savior, have called us to be children of the light. Change our lenses so we might not only see others and ourselves more accurately but also so we might lift our eyes (lamps) and focus on you. Amen.

Oops, I've Fallen

We definitely live in a fallen world. Why, just today I was attacked by a doll. Not just any doll but one of my own. I had her standing on my dresser top, and when I bent over to slide open a drawer, she fell and beaned me on my noggin. Her head is porcelain while mine, I thought, was granite. Evidently my noodle is more the consistency of Silly Putty, because her head left a crater-sized indentation in my cranium. She came down with such a thud it took me several minutes before I could carry on.

Speaking of noodles, get this. In Japan a noodle museum is all the rage. Honest. It's far more popular than the art museums, which are generally visited only by scholars.

Imagine if someone could combine the two. The "Mona Lisa" could be done in rigatoni (be hard for her not to smirk). Or picture "Whistler's Mother" trying to rock on a chair of macaroni. (Next we'll be sticking a feathered hat on her.) Or how about "The Girl with the Watering Can" being renamed "The Girl with the Ravioli."

Actually, the noodle museum is dedicated to the ramen noodle, which I understand is as popular in Japan as hot dogs are at Chicago's O'Hare Airport (more are sold there than anywhere else in the country). In one year the Japanese wolf down enough noodles at the museum's nine ramen shops to encircle the globe five times. Wow! Imagine if it rained. It could give new meaning to wet noodle — although if it filled in the ozone hole that could be good.

I think the news proves daily how off our noodles we humans are. Our fallen condition is proclaimed continuously by our odd behavior. I think of individuals who have been featured on the ten o'clock news for scaling high-rise buildings in major cities. The Andes are one thing, but the World Trade Center? C'mon, what's that about? Or skydiving off the Space Needle. Spacey, if you ask me. But then, truth be known, I've done a few weird things myself.

I remember the time I wound my foot around my neck (I was much younger) in an attempt to duplicate a trick by a TV contortionist. I managed to slide my foot around the back of my neck, but when my toes hooked close to my ear, I couldn't unwind myself. It took just seconds to realize what an unnatural position this was so I yelled to my husband for help.

To suggest Les was amazed when he tromped into the room and saw his wife in a virtual knot would be to underestimate his incredulous response. "Hurry," I commanded, hoping to jolt him into action. It worked, and he dislodged my foot, releasing the pressure off my cramping leg. I appreciated his assistance but was a tad irritated at his incessant snickering during the unwinding process.

Of course, I remember the time Les fell two stories off a roof with two bundles of roofing tiles on his shoulder. Falling off a roof is not odd. What was odd was when he stood up after several moments of staring at the sky, picked up the bundles, and scaled his way back up to the roof to finish the job.

If it isn't dolls falling on us and knocking us silly, our own silly fascinations remind us that sometimes we let life get out of whack. All that points to our fallen nature. We just can't keep things in balance (or balanced on our dresser tops).

When in doubt about your need to be saved, just check what's out of place in your life. It could be decorations that won't stay put, interests that become fetishes, or some less-than-bright action you've taken. Fortunately, even if something falls on our noodle or if we fall on our behind, God's everlasting arms pick us up, and he embraces us with his loving-kindness.

I don't know for sure, Lord, but I think we might be confused by your call for us to become peculiar people. We are fallen people with strange ways. Please deliver us from our bright ideas. Untie our noodley brains lest we become wise in our own eyes. Amen.

Bridging the Gap

For I am convinced that neither death nor life,
neither angels nor demons, neither the present
nor the future, nor any powers, neither height nor depth,
nor anything else in all creation, will be able
to separate us from the love of God that is in
Christ Jesus our Lord.
ROMANS 8:38–39

I love to tour other people's homes. Actually, I love to tour other people's lives. And I have been known to be an incessant interviewer with those whom I meet along life's way. Sometimes my interviewees seem a tad reluctant, but I don't discourage easily. Because of this tell-me-all-you-know gene of mine, I even enjoy snooping through other's homes and lives on the TV Home and Garden channel.

On a recent program, a well-seasoned Michigan couple showed their lovely 1800s restored home. What really caught my attention was an activity they were involved in that was casually mentioned. Each morning at 6:30 this duo sets off on a frisky jaunt to prepare for the traditional walk across the Mackinac Bridge, which they have been taking part in for years.

The dedicated pair pace off two-and-a-half miles each morning for months prior to Memorial Day (bridge day) to build their stamina. In fact, they were so consistent in their practice walks that neighbors could set their clocks by the couple. By the time the holiday arrived, they were ready to join thousands of other folks for the big crossing.

One reason this couple captured my attention is because I'm a rousing Michigan native. Yeah, Michigan! But more importantly, I have a deep appreciation for that bridge because it led me and kept me connected to Les prior to our marriage. I lived in a suburb of Detroit in the bottom of the Lower Peninsula, and Les lived in a tiny town at the top of the Upper Peninsula. The Mackinac Bridge united the Upper and Lower Peninsulas, and us. Yeah, bridge!

Since marrying, Les and I have crossed the Mackinac Bridge more than a hundred times on our treks to visit family. We too traverse the expanse via foot — that's with Les's right foot firmly pressed on the pedal of our van's accelerator. We have often scurried across the five-mile bridge in anticipation of seeing family on the other side.

This famous bridge arches over the spot where Lakes Huron and Michigan merge. If you throw a quarter over one side, your money will be deposited in the Huron while a coin off the other side ends up officially in Lake Michigan. Hmm, the bridge brought together two lakes, two peninsulas, two sweethearts, and two families. No wonder I'm fond of this stretch of metal girders, cables, and highway.

An even greater expanse separates earth and heaven. Christ became our bridge to God. Christ offers us daily assistance, divine opportunities, and eternal provision. He also extends to us his Word, which allows us to arch over this world's distorted mind-set to receive the pure wisdom that is from above.

Speaking of bridges, what about prayer? In quiet conversations with our Lord, we hear in our longing hearts of his expansive love, which helps us to move from our inner conflict to his peaceful resolution.

As if that weren't enough, he allows people who are sometimes as disconnected from each other as two peninsulas to be united by the bridge of forgiveness.

What gap yawns before you? What provision has God made to span that distance and to bring together that which has been separated by sin, time, and emotional distance? What do you need to do to avail yourself of that provision?

Dear Lord, thank you for bridging heaven and earth, for without you our feet of clay would be stuck in earth's mire. Tour our hearts even if we seem reluctant, and help us to be faithful bridge walkers. In fact, Lord, wouldn't it be something if others could set their watches by our daily exemplary lives? May we show that kind of dedication and preparation. We realize that one day — one memorable day — we will finally cross over to the other side to be eternally united with you. To that we say, "Yeah, Lord!" Amen.

Masterpiece

He who began a good work in you will carry it on
to completion until the day of Christ Jesus.
PHILIPPIANS 1:6

One of the featured art pieces at the J. Paul Getty Museum in Los Angeles is *Prayerbook for a Queen: The Hours of Jeanne d'Evreux.* This tiny, artistic masterpiece, on loan to the museum, was a gift to the queen of France seven hundred years ago. Only three-and-a-half-inches-high by two-and-a-half-inches-wide, the prayer book consists of painted vellum pages. Part of what distinguishes the Getty display is that the book's leaves have been removed from the binding to photograph each page, allowing nearly sixty pages to be displayed for public viewing as opposed to the usual two. Two dozen full-scale illuminations from the book, done by miniaturist Jean Pucelle, are now visible for museum-goers.

Imagine having your prayer book considered historical and worthy of people lining up to view it. Today many of us keep tabs on our prayer lives through journals in which we write our concerns, feelings, and activities, culminating in a prayer that might be two lines or two pages long. Some of us diligently keep both a life journal, in which we record life's events and our feelings, and a prayer journal, which consists of our requests and praises offered up to our Father.

Now, I stated that as if to suggest I do, which isn't accurate. I'm an occasional scribbler of thought and prayer, not a daily one. Oh, I pray daily; I just don't record daily. In fact, for years my personal scribbles were done on the backs of envelopes, napkins, and old receipts. Wouldn't that be great museum fodder? They could be displayed in a bushel basket. Perhaps they could be called "Patsy's Paltry Prayers." Although, good news, today I have advanced to a leather journal. My last entry, though, was two months ago; so you don't have to worry about my trying to send you on any guilt trip. (I'd have to buy my own ticket first.)

Luci, on the other hand, has kept exquisite journals for years. Hers truly are worthy of public viewing—if they weren't so personal. She is an artist with an eye for placement, and her printing is elegant. Her own art (sketches, watercolors, colored pencil) dots the landscape of her journals as do photographs and other memorabilia. Perhaps seven hundred years from now (surely Jesus will come for us before then), Luci's work, like the queen's, will be carefully offered for public scrutiny. I know I would line up to see it. (I would be only 753 years old.)

As I considered the queen's book, I couldn't help thinking about the King's book, the Bible. Now there is a journal if I ever saw one. Talk about exquisite, have you read David's psalms lately? Open up to a page and read afresh the sweet songs of a young shepherd, hear the cries of a pursued warrior, and the anguish of a repentant king. From the pause in pastures, to pleas for pardon, to peals of praise, the account is David's journey; it's his prayer book. Amazingly enough, it's available for public viewing.

Talk about art, the Song of Solomon, the book of Ruth, and the creation account paint vivid pictures on the canvas of our hearts. Each word from the Scriptures, like brush strokes, allows us breathtaking views all the way from Mount Nebo, to Calvary, to the Emmaus Road, and finally to the crystal river flowing from God's throne. The prophetic utterances of Ezekiel, Daniel, and Revelation render art almost beyond our imagining. And don't miss the musings of King Solomon in the Proverbs, Hagar's heartrending struggles, the eloquence of the Sermon on the Mount, or Paul's dramatic shipwrecks.

Imagine all of this and more — much, much more. No waiting in line to view this life-changing masterpiece. In fact, if your home is like mine, you have several choices of Bibles. Let's not let them become museum pieces or dust collectors. Instead, let's daily invest ourselves in the pages that we might become true works of art at the hands of the Creator.

Dear Author and Finisher of our faith, thank you that you will complete the (art) work you have begun in us. May you transform us into pleasing renderings of your exquisite beauty. Amen.

Lost and Found

Christ in you, the hope of glory.
COLOSSIANS 1:27

Keep this under your hat: Paradise Lost has been found. No kidding, Les and I have found our Shangrila. At every turn, we see breathtaking vistas of rocky ranges, flowered borders, and peach sunsets. Palm trees dance in celebration, swishing their fronds like feather dusters in the sky. And bougainvillea cascades across the landscape, climbing, draping, and spilling down walls. A profusion of gardens, fountains, and pools bring soothing, visual refreshment. The evening sky, like a great dome, surrounds us in a spectacular display of illumination. Even the mountains daily shout strength and beauty. Ah, yes, paradise, Palm Desert, California.

I don't know about you, but I'm susceptible to viewing the lives of others from afar and believing their existence is easier, calmer, and more meaningful than mine — rather paradisiacal. Not all the time, mind you, but I do have those moments when I give way to envy because I'm trudging through a dreary season while someone else seems to be skipping down a well-lit path. But I guess peeking over the fence at the greener grass is part of our human tendency. I mean, consider some of these folks . . .

Sarah of Genesis fame felt God was tardy fulfilling his promises to her regarding a baby. So she thought she would assist him. Sarah had trudged through many seasons waiting for a child and had since entered midlife, which doused her fruitful hopes. But Sarah took a peek at Hagar her servant, and hark, Hagar was like a skipping roe. In Sarah's mind, her sweet servant girl would be just the right choice to bear her husband's child on Sarah's behalf.

Wrong! Paradise turned into "Big-Time Wrestling" when Hagar began to tout her success and Sarah began to shout her disapproval. Sarah was offended. Abraham was saddened. And Hagar was expelled from their midst. Alas, seems Sarah was better off before she started helping God out.

King Ahab had incredible riches and power. But when he looked over the fence and saw his neighbor's yard, Ahab knew he had to own that plot of land. Why, anyone could see it was the ideal place for the king's garden. Well, almost anyone—just not the owner, who wasn't the least bit interested in selling. Ahab broke out into a big-time case of the pouts. The queen, in her attempt to give her whining husband everything he wanted (paradise), had the neighbor bumped off. But planting the seeds of disdain in any ground will only bring forth disaster. Ask King Ahab or Queen Jezebel. In fact, you may want to examine for yourself their dogged trail of regret (in 1 Kings 22:34–37 and 2 Kings 9:30–37). Hmm, if only they had been satisfied with what they already had.

Oh, yeah, about Les's and my paradise, did I mention the sand? Oh, well, it's everywhere. When the winds whip, the sand permeates the condo even though the doors and windows are closed tightly. And the winds sometimes become so vengeful it causes the entire valley to howl like a dust bowl. This winter a swirling wind tore out sixty trees near us—very near us, outside our door.

Then there's the heat and lack of humidity that leaves one's body withering for moisture. And the screeching night frogs that sound like a woman's screams for help. Not to mention the black widow spiders, the legions of grasshoppers, and the earthquakes. Well, there goes paradise, lost again.

Some sand and wind will come into everyone's life, no matter how perfect it seems. Remember screaming Sarah, who was almost blown away in her attempts to have things her way. And withering Ahab, who tripped himself up when his sandals filled with another man's sandy soil.

Keep this under your hat (where your brains are) and in your heart (where hope abides): "In this life we shall have tribulations . . ." Paradise? That comes later.

Lord, may we be grateful for all you have given us. Would you please guard our hearts against envy and from our own self-serving agendas? Thank you for the promise of a future paradise. May we wait expectantly and patiently. Amen.

Pictures of Grace

We bring nothing to God, and He gives us everything.
GARY THOMAS

What picture comes to mind when you hear the word *grace?* I think of a woman named — what else — Grace, who lived near our family's home when I was growing up. She and her husband were friends of my parents and, believe me, that's where the friendship ended. Grace had no, uh, grace for children. She and her husband didn't have little ones of their own so perhaps that's why Grace had no space in her heart for me.

Of course, I was a precocious pip-squeak, quite full of myself. I was a second child, the first girl, who arrived in our family after a nine-year interval. That gave me some distinct advantages, of which I took full advantage. Grace evidently struggled with my indulged ways. I too struggled . . . with Grace.

Years later, in desperate hours of my life, I experienced another grace: God's grace. The Lord gave me a place to stand in his presence — me, the precocious kid, now a confused adult. I couldn't believe he had space in his heart for me. This undeserved reception and inclusion stunned me. And, honestly, I struggled . . . with grace.

Two distinct pictures of "grace." One portrays not even a smidgen of favor or friendly regard; the other speaks of lavish acceptance. I had trouble with both.

I couldn't bear the feelings I had when I was in Grace's home. I felt physically rigid and certain that if I bumped anything or dropped something my life expectancy would be reduced drastically. Yet what troubled me most wasn't just the sense that I might do something wrong but the feeling I *was* something wrong.

God's grace, which gave me the freedom to be myself without condemnation, was not only foreign but also a little frightening. I was used to trying to win approval and not receiving it until I had performed some necessary stunts, like making my bed, saying my prayers, and attending church thirty-three times a week. Unmerited favor is hard to swallow, and yet, when received, it sweetly quenches my deep thirst for unconditional love.

A third picture of grace comes to my mind—the grace depicted in a painting of an iris. Actually two paintings: one portrays beds of this lovely, elegant flower; the other a single iris. When you view these famous works of art, you see only the flowers; you have no sense of their location. Are they in a city park, a flowered field, or perhaps on a rambling farm?

There's a reason for the mystery. Not only does the artist's selective focus keep us from being distracted by peripheral objects, we also aren't alerted to the artist's real world. The painter, Vincent van Gogh, created his masterpieces in an asylum.

In some of the darkest hours of his life, van Gogh found a single, graceful flower, and he made that his focus. His outside world at the asylum was grim at best, and everything around him was a reminder of his internal sadness. Yet somehow van Gogh, when he saw the irises, was able to connect himself to the only lovely thing in his surroundings. Captured by the flowers' gracefulness, he painted them several times. Yet it is believed he never found the inner grace or peace he was searching for. He never saw beyond the purple iris to its providential Designer. He struggled . . . with grace.

I too have seen grace in God's creations — a swan gliding across a still pond, a gazelle leaping across an African plain, an eagle soaring above a craggy cliff. As effortless as those movements are, so is the ease with which God bestows his extravagant gift of grace into our lives.

Grace is stunning. It is breathtaking. It is more beautiful than van Gogh's *Irises*. Grace finds us in our poverty and presents us with the gift of an inheritance we didn't deserve . . . the gift of grace.

Grace to you and peace from God our Father and the Lord Jesus Christ.

PHILEMON 1:3

4x4 . . . and I'm Not Talking My Hip Size

Amazing grace! How sweet the sound.
JOHN NEWTON

My spiffy new jalopy was parked in the driveway just waiting for me to unwrap it. It was the first new car I had picked out all by myself (like a big girl). A petite, sage-colored 4x4, the vehicle was equipped to take on the unsettled weather of Michigan and had just enough space in the back for my husband's electric cart that shuttled him effortlessly around malls and grocery stores. Les nicknamed his cart the Aarp Express, Aarpy, for short—referring to his card-carrying status as a member in the American Association of Retired Persons (AARP). I hadn't named my car yet.

When Les left on a week-long trip, my snappy wheels and I remained behind to get acquainted. I had only driven the vehicle a couple times. When Sunday morning rolled around, the day was frosty and flaky, and I headed out to drive my little darling to church. I started her up, and she purred like a kitten. What a sweet sound. After finally figuring out how to adjust my seat and strap on my seat belt, I tackled the defroster. This is when our relationship began to chill.

I couldn't find the right button. I did locate the sunroof button. About a quarter inch of fresh snow accumulated on my hairdo before I refound the sunroof button and shut the thing. But I couldn't find where the sick-o who designed the car had hidden my defroster button. Finally, using my fingernails, I scraped a four-by-six-inch opening on the windshield, turned on my wipers (which wouldn't stay on), and, grumbling, slid out of the driveway.

Within two blocks my four-by-six porthole had shrunk to a one-by-one peephole. I turned into a driveway to regroup (murmur, murmur). From the glove compartment I fished out the owner's manual. Printed across the book's cover in large letters was this message: "Read Manual Before Operating Vehicle." (Groan.)

That's the bottom line, folks: if we don't know how to unwrap and operate what we have, it will be of little value to us. We will be sidelined and left to fumble for the right buttons to push. I could tell from the outside that I had acquired a classy chassis, but I didn't understand the inside workings, which were vital to me if I was to benefit from all the vehicle had to offer.

The same is true of understanding God's workings. If we're not intimately familiar with his manual, what are the chances we'll understand his ways? Even reading the manual doesn't guarantee we'll comprehend the mystery of his plans, but at least we'll have a handle on which buttons to push in this life and which ones to avoid.

The Book will also help us to grasp grace as we study those who have gone before us. Living examples are some of the best learning aids. Take Abigail . . .

Old Testament Abby boarded her trusty, four-hoofed vehicle (her desert donkey) and headed out of her driveway. She wasn't on her way to church. Instead, she was bound for a colossal confrontation. Abigail was about to stand against 401 armed vigilantes who were on their way to her home to kill every man on the compound. This intelligent woman, who obviously had read the manual carefully, faced her enemies with courage and amazing grace — and turned them into friends. Abigail said all the right things. No grumbles, no groans, no murmurs. Imagine if she had pushed even one wrong button on those already outraged men. Why, Abby could have been their first casualty.

If you want an inside view of grace, if you want to see how to unwrap this astounding gift, take a closer look at Abigail, Hannah, Lydia, and Anna (whose very name means *grace*), and many of the other sisters who embraced grace long before we toddled onto the scene. Reading the manual makes sense. For who knows when loved ones may leave us, when winter may set in with a vengeance, or when enemies may pursue us, and we will need to know the sweet sounds of amazing grace.

Oh, by the way, I named my vehicle "Sassy."

The grace of the Lord Jesus be with you.
1 CORINTHIANS 16:23

No Guts, No Glory

Grace under pressure.
ERNEST HEMINGWAY

"Grace under pressure" was Hemingway's response when someone asked him what he meant by the word *guts*.

What an elegant definition for such a sweaty, life-wrenching word. I tend to think of a word like *grace* as a woman's word, and a word like *guts* as a guy's word. But the truth is, Mike Utley was a picture of grace when he faced the toughest tackle life could challenge him with, and he stood to take another step.

Les and I sat with our eyes glued to the television as the big, strapping ex-football player took hold of the fore-arms of two of his teammates, using them as balance bars. With their help and his determination, he stood to his feet and prepared to take his first step in seven years. The man, Mike Utley, had been injured in a football game. Since severely damaging, but not severing, his spinal cord, he fought his way back to health. Seven years of grueling physical therapy. Seven years of maintaining an "I can do it" attitude.

I remember when Mike was carried out on a stretcher, and I remember breathing a prayer on his behalf. Les and I followed up on news reports about Mike's injury until, after a time, more current events filled the airways. Then our own challenges filled our minds and, quite honestly, we hadn't thought about Mike for a long time. But when the newscast showed him taking his first step, we watched in admiration as Mike dedicated himself to the task before him. Jaw set, eyes focused on his goal, with support people in place around him, the giant clutched his friends, and with tremendous courage and all the guts he could muster, he took his step. Exhausted from the effort, he was lowered back into a wheelchair. What a gutsy man!

Our willingness to embrace grace is more difficult when it's depicted in such a costly manner. But grace wasn't the injury Mike sustained; the injury was simply life's parcel. Grace was Mike's ability to accept wherever life took him and to continue to move forward.

This grace was evident in Joseph's life as well. Joseph was rejected and abandoned by his brothers, then falsely accused and imprisoned by his employer. He sat forgotten in jail for years. What a potential breeding ground for hostility, resentment, and anger! But instead of steeping in self-pity or seething in indignation, Joseph became an exemplary prisoner and a trusted leader in the jail. Forgotten by others, but not by God, Joseph was granted unmerited favor in his captors' eyes. Eventually, Joseph was released and elevated to the second highest in command over Egypt.

I believe God's fortitude and grace sustain the Josephs and the Mikes, the Josephines and the Michelles of this world. Even the Patsys.

For I too was a prisoner, an emotional prisoner. For several years I was held hostage in my home by fear and anger. Not knowing how to deal with the inequities of life, I stuffed my splintered emotions. Unlike Mike or Joseph, I wasn't courageous, nor did I know how to handle life's pressures. Still, in my extreme weakness, God extended his grace to me. I embraced grace like a balance bar and gradually got back on my feet. Then with my jaw set and my eyes focused, I took the first gutsy steps out of my home.

God wants you to experience his grace whether you have faced your life with courage or with cowardice. Grace is not about us; it is about God. He will meet you wherever you are to help you take the next gutsy step. Understanding God's grace and appreciating it will change your approach to life's pressures. You will begin to see the injustices as opportunities for you to watch God at work.

By the way, God is not often in a hurry to move us on before we benefit deeply from our experiences. So don't be disheartened when others forget your long, hard struggles. He will never forget . . . and his grace will exalt you in due time.

You then . . . be strong in the grace that is in Christ Jesus. . . . Endure hardship with us like a good soldier of Christ Jesus.

2 TIMOTHY 2:1, 3

A Little Whine with Your Cheese?

Grace, indeed, is beauty in action.
DISRAELI

Sick takes grace. No, let me restate that. Doing sick well takes grace. I personally don't do sick well. I whine well. (Everyone has her strengths.) Actually, I excel in the art of whining.

I learned to whine as the baby girl in our family line. That is, until I was thirteen, and then my sister was born, and I had to grow up . . . a little. After thirteen years of whining, though, I had established a response pattern that was hard to shake. Ask my husband. No, on second thought, don't.

To whine well you must learn to make your words singsong to the tune of, say, a dirge. Then you must drag out your syllables: "I don't waan-nahhh." You may want to practice that. Emphasis and drama play key roles in the act of being truly nauseating. Body language is also important to convey an all-over whine: Shoulders should slump forward, head should wag, and whatever you do, don't forget the lip. The bottom one must protrude about three inches, heading south toward your shuffling feet. Are you getting the picture? Pretty, huh? After you've mastered the art, plan on spending a lot of time alone.

Oh, did I fail to mention that one of the side effects of being a whiner is people tire of you pronto? That response gives the whiner something new to — what else — whine about. So if you're going to be a serious whiner, it will help if you like the sound of your own voice.

By the way, the higher your voice's octave, the more annoying it will be to others. That can be temporarily effective, but I must warn you that long term it may decrease your life expectancy. Folks can be so intolerant.

Of course, "silent whining" is also very effective. The silence screams, "Look at me, notice me, fix my unhappiness!" This type of whiner is able to manage entire households without a word. Often you'll find her sitting in her room alone for days, waiting to be rescued by some guilt-ridden relative. Such whiners gravitate toward rocking chairs. The type with squeaks are the most appealing so the whiner can send a cranky lullaby throughout the dwelling. Voiceless whiners are the ones who slam cupboards and doors to make a point and then, when confronted, swear that nothing is bothering them.

Grace has a very different look (whew). Soft like down, gentle like a summer breeze. Its sound is a rippling brook, a sparrow's song, a hymn of praise. Grace wears well. It is chiffon, it is silk, it is gossamer. Others welcome grace, like a sister, a friend, a Savior. Grace moves with the ease of a monarch butterfly and the lilt of a leaf pirouetting toward the earth. Grace curtsies. Grace is polite, spacious, and richly endowed. Grace bows to serve and reigns with mercy.

Whiners neither enjoy nor give joy. But grace-filled people are reputable, sought after, and deeply loved. They stand heads above others even while on their knees. They are full of forgiveness and wisdom. You often find them nurturing children, caring for the ill, serving the underprivileged, applauding the successes of others, and celebrating God's generosity.

Grace is Ruth of the Bible, bent over in the scorching fields to feed herself and her mother-in-law. Grace is Naomi embracing Ruth's baby as if it were her own. Grace is Abigail, facedown in the dirt before David as an advocate for her workers. It is Esther, kneeling before the king on behalf of a nation. It is Hagar, returning submissively to her angered employer. It is Hannah, turning her young son Samuel over to the priest Eli, as she promised. Grace is a young virgin who cried, "Be it unto me according to thy word" (Luke 1:38 KJV).

Yes, grace knows how to suffer well . . . and how to live well. Do we?

All beautiful you are, my darling; there is no flaw in you.

SONG OF SONGS 4:7

Dressed to Kill

God's grace is the oil that fills the lamp of love.
HENRY WARD BEECHER

Today Les and I lunched at a charming French café. It was a delicious day, the kind you want to go on forever. The weather was perfect with enough warmth to sizzle and enough breeze to soothe. The food was scrumptious, and our table was situated outside under a wide striped awning. Music danced among the patrons, encircling us with cheery French sentiments. We drank in our surroundings of mountains in the distance, palm trees, and people nearby. Les and I chatted casually while we applauded the flaky French pastries and mused over the birds that dined on crumbs at our feet. We were delighted with the Paris ambiance, and we were pleased with each other.

Eventually, I decided to walk down the street to visit a couple of my favorite gift shops. (I have several in each city and in each state of the Union.) Les agreed to meet me in about thirty minutes at a certain store.

As I made my way to one of "my" shops, I realized the temperature was rising. The material of my beige outfit was a little weighty, and I was feeling the heat.

Then something caught my eye: a display of cool summer outfits surrounded by snappy accessories. The next thing I knew I had drifted inside and was trying them on. Wouldn't you know it? I looked darling. In fact, I was so cute I had the saleswoman clip all the tags off the outfit so I could wear it out the door. I then spotted a chipper yellow hat that would just top off the look, so I added it to the bill.

As I passed other store windows on my way to meet my husband, I caught sight of my new reflection and giggled, imagining Les's reaction.

I sashayed into the store and spotted Les chatting with the owner. Les glanced in my direction and started to turn away when something told him to look again. His head swiveled back and, as he took another gander, an incredulous look galloped across his face as he realized I was his beloved lunch date, the woman he thought he knew.

Oh, did I fail to mention that the outfit's screaming vibrancy made me look like an escapee from Ringling Brothers? Either that or I had bumped into a nauseated clown. Also, I don't wear hats.

I wish I could have recorded that moment. Les did decide to keep me, and I'm grateful.

Isn't that what happens so often in relationships? Just when we think we have someone figured out, she changes. Change is often startling, even scary. Yet many times, it's good. Change can be confusing too. We think, *Why would anyone change when everything seemed to be going so well?* And change is usually jarring. I think change takes grace for all involved, because even the most positive kinds of change, uh, change things.

I remember when I first made a personal commitment to Christ, my decision changed me in many ways. While most of those changes pleased my husband, some of my new behavior and beliefs annoyed him. Suddenly I didn't appreciate Les's colorful humor, and he didn't appreciate my judgmental attitude. I didn't like his beer (and all it represented), and he didn't like my control issues. I stopped smoking and decided he should too. He decided I should mind my own business.

I desperately needed God's grace for my deficient life, and I needed to experience grace to know how to extend it to others—like my beloved husband. When a person changes, it takes time for those around her to adjust and figure out what that means to their relationship. We complicate the adjustment to our change when we insist on trying to take everyone with us. Truth is, we can't change other people; only God can do that.

We can, though, extend grace to them. Grace is the space that allows others to grow or not grow, to agree or disagree, to change or remain unchanged. No wonder grace is a gift from God; left on our own, we humans just don't have that kind of spacious room inside us.

When we understand the great value in grace, then even when those around us show up dressed to kill, we won't. Instead, we will share the gift that God has so graciously bestowed upon us.

We have this treasure in jars of clay to show that this all-surpassing power is from God.

2 CORINTHIANS 4:7

Oh, Poor Baby

The grace you had yesterday won't do for today.
OSWALD CHAMBERS

My mom, Rebecca, grew up on a Kentucky farm. She was the youngest of six children and was nicknamed "Sister." (I guess their nicknaming creativity ran thin by number six, or perhaps because my mom was such a petite munchkin, "Sister" just seemed to fit her.)

Mom told me that her family never had a lot of material possessions, but they were well fed because they ate from the farm's bounty. When the Great Depression hit, they didn't feel the impact to the degree that many others did because they worked for themselves and could rely on their crops. But they knew all about putting in a hard day's work in the fields. They also suffered painful loss when my grandmother died, leaving behind a young, grieving family.

During my grandmother's lingering illness, a woman of prayer stopped by for a visit. My mother was seated nearby when the woman noticed that Sister's little-girl hands were covered in hundreds of warts. The woman called my mother to her side and embraced her hands. At one point the woman stroked Mom's hands and said, "Oh, poor baby . . . oh, poor baby." Clasping them once more in her own hands, the woman said her good-byes and left.

Over the next several days the warts began to fall off my mother's hands until, within a week, all the warts were gone, never to return.

Many times my mom has retold this story to me. She said the woman didn't say she was praying while she touched Mom's hands, but my mother sensed it even at her young age. Mom believes that the Lord answered this woman's prayers and healed a little girl's hands.

I'm impressed that the woman touched my mother's hands and embraced them with such tenderness. Often, I find, when people aren't as we think they should be, we tend to withdraw—which is a hoot when we realize almost nothing in this life is without flaw. But our human nature is to pull back physically, emotionally, and relationally when we encounter defects in another. We don't always know how to respond to what seems abnormal to us—unless, like the woman of prayer, we have experienced God's grace for the abnormalities in our own lives. For I believe God's grace enables us not to be alarmed, frightened, or repelled at humankind's defectiveness.

This story also reminds me that ministry to others doesn't have to be announced or showy. The woman never said, "Kneel, child, I'm about to pray." Yet my mother sensed the woman's spirit of faith as well as her merciful approach. I believe this woman had experienced God's grace in her life, for we can't give away to others something we don't have.

The story of Anna, whose very name means "grace," is found in the New Testament. She experienced God's grace when she became a widow after only seven years of marriage. We know that loss has the potential to cause us to shrivel or shine depending on how we embrace our sadness and his provision. Anna became a noted woman of prayer, praise, and prophecy and remained faithful more than eighty years in this ministry until she beheld the Christ child. Anna shone.

A grace-filled woman is one who extends herself to others with sensitivity, mercy, good taste, and insight. Anna and the woman of prayer in my mother's life spent much time in God's grace-filled presence. That's why a "sister" could sense the spirit of prayer operative in one life and how, in the other, Anna could live alone for eighty years and still shine brightly for the Lord.

Maybe this explains why my light is flickery, why my well of mercy is more like a puddle than a pool, why good taste and sensitivity are sometimes erased by my reactive personality, and why my insights vary in value. I, for one, need to get down on my knees and not get up until I embrace more of his extravagant grace.

Let us then approach the throne of grace with confidence, so that we may receive mercy and find grace to help us in our time of need.

Shine, Shine, Shine!

The older Les and I become the more we appreciate a well-lit path. We want to see where we're going as we bop from one room to another. (In the past, we've tripped over everything from vacuum cleaners to each other.) We also want light to see what we're reading without straining our bifocals or our brains. And we want to see to measure ingredients during our sporadic kitchen escapades—and I do mean sporadic.

The exception to this illuminating need in our lives would be the lighting around our morning mirror, the bedtime mirror, and, oh, yes, the daytime mirror. Some things are better left in the shadows.

Recently Les purchased some solar lights to place along our walkways and our patio. I was fascinated. These clever illuminators gather light during the day, store it, then shine like crazy at night. This eliminates the need for unsightly wires and electricity. These lamps are spiffy.

One night, high winds blew a couple of these lights off their pedestals and ping-ponged them around our patio. So Les brought them in and laid them on our dresser. Later, when I entered the dark bedroom, the pool of light emanating from the room's corner startled me.

Even during off-hours they continued to shine, shine, shine. Reminded me of the song "This Little Light of Mine."

Being touched by God's extravagant grace ignites something within us that causes others to notice. It's an interior glow that is like an exterior light in that it casts its influence in spite of the degree of darkness in which it finds itself—not only in spite of the darkness but also because of it. In the darkness the light becomes more attractive, more influential, more valuable, and more obvious.

Deborah, a judge in the Old Testament, was called to be a solar light during a time when spiritual darkness covered the land. She rose to the call, took a stand for truth, and stayed faithful even in the face of an intimidating enemy. God used this woman's life to redirect an entire nation's steps. Previously, the people were stumbling around in the darkness of their own poor choices, straining to walk in their own piteous ways, and measuring their behavior by their neighbors' behavior. They definitely needed a well-lit path; they needed some solar lights. Then Deborah, who gathered brilliance in God's presence, became his light-holder and his light-bearer—and she did it with strength and grace.

I've seen this type of dedication in my friend Thelma. She is a light-bearer of the brightest kind. Thelma has a bottomless reservoir of God's love for people that she lavishly sprinkles around. I enjoy watching Thelma's beaming face as she embraces the ladies in her hug lines at conferences. She enfolds folks in acceptance and guides them to our radiant Savior and his illuminating counsel. I've watched Thelma send forth his light and shine, shine, shine.

I've also observed when Thelma has faced difficult days, times when the Prince of Darkness has tried to trip her up, and she has reached even deeper into her arsenal of God's light-giving truth. Thelma is a solar light who faithfully stores light while it is day. I have benefited from seeing the commitment in her life, for while Thelma is capable of feisty, what you see is faithful because of God's grace aglow in her soul. You shine, girl-friend!

What does it take to be a solar-powered sister? A relationship with Christ, a dedication to his Word, and God's brilliant grace. If you need greater clarification in your life, if you're uncertain what next step you should take, if you long to make a difference in your world, then invite Christ to bring the light of his life into your darkened understanding. If you've done that and still feel as if you're stumbling around, then redouble your efforts to be in his light-bearing Word. Gather up his truth, store it in your heart, and then shine like crazy.

Each one should use whatever gift he has received to serve others, faithfully administering God's grace in its various forms.

1 PETER 4:10

Surprise!

Afflictions are often the black folds in which
God doth set the jewels of his children's graces,
to make them shine better.

CHARLES SPURGEON

What a surprise that the Lord would lavish us with his favor!

I still become almost giddy at the thought that today I am an author. It makes me giggle to even write the word *author.* I had wanted to write ever since I was a child, but I took a sharp left turn out the school's front door at age sixteen, when I quit school, and veered right into trouble.

After years of flailing about, I stepped onto God's narrow path and into his wide swath of grace. His path eventually led me into — surprise! — writing.

Another grace gift came to me packaged in blue. I'll never forget when I unwrapped the bundle of blankets tucked around my eldest son and found inside a miracle. I couldn't believe that God could bring forth good out of my damaged life, much less a black-haired, brown-eyed squirming wonder. For me, Marty's birth was a sign of God's favor, unmerited by me.

But it doesn't take a lot of living to discover that all of life's surprises aren't worthy of a party. The first smack of reality starts at birth with a firm whack (surprise!) across our backsides, which should prepare us for the jolts ahead. Yet life continues to catch us off guard with those moments that cause us to reel.

I'm telling you, life can be a blessing . . . and life can be brutal.

When I was thirteen, I was the pitcher for a neighborhood baseball game. I took a line drive (surprise!) right to my throat. Ah, but here's the good news: I threw the bum out at first base before I collapsed. So there!

I still can recall in living color another time when blood gushed from my knees after I catapulted myself into the air at an amazing speed, all because I attempted to stop my bicycle by squeezing both hand brakes hard. How was I to know (surprise!) that "easy" goes a long way? It was my maiden voyage.

My youngest son, Jason, will not forget the day Mom slammed the car door (surprise!) on his fingers. In my overstated way, I gave the door the old heave-ho and, much to my horror and his, smashed Jason's fingers. I was grateful no digits were broken, just a piece of my heart to think I could have brought pain to his little life.

In blessings we expect to find God's generous grace. Yet his grace is also extended to us in brutal moments. In fact, I have found that, like a diamond bracelet presented on a square of black velvet, some of the most exquisite presentations of this merciful attribute of God's are often in the dark hours of our soul.

When the batter hit me with that baseball, I wanted to hurt him. Well, at least his pride. I savored the umpire's cry of, "You're out!" But I'm grateful the Lord doesn't respond that way to me. For how many times have I hurt the Lord with my retaliatory attitude? My instant response may be to get even with the other guy, only then to experience God's willingness to embrace me despite my insolence.

My hubby and I are feisty folks and given to disputes. But the Lord has huddled with Les and me in our "time-outs" like a referee to help us become more gracious with each other.

Sometimes I've caused myself pain, but the Lord has picked up this scuffed maiden and set my feet back on solid ground. Sometimes I've felt bruised by my own expectations of others, and sometimes, in my rush, I've made poor judgment calls. And how often, in my negligence, have I, like a child going out to play, slammed my heart's door closed, only to have grace flood in a window?

Hmm, perhaps I've been wrong. Most events in our lives might well be worthy of calling up friends to join in a celebration. For, on careful scrutiny, we find that God's grace-filled fingerprints are all over our lives. Surprise!

The grace of our Lord was poured out on me abundantly.

1 TIMOTHY 1:14

Day by Day

If God only made his presence known in the momentous,
how barren our lives would be
of grace-filled windows to the sacred.

DEBRA KLINGSPORN

I stood in the grocery store checkout lane and watched the cashier's fingers race over the number pads while the register tape spewed forth. For a moment, as the tape stretched out and then began to curl up, it reminded me of my life.

At this juncture I have tallied more days than I can believe. They seem to have raced along, and often there was a price I paid. Now when I'm asked my age I have to stop to figure it out (duh). I'm surprised to find that the accumulation of days is so hefty and that my children are established adults.

As I write, it is March, the month of the lion and the lamb. I'm amazed because it seems as though New Year's Day was just last week. March. Hmm, that means nine weeks have passed, sixty-three days since the year began.

What did I spend those days on? Let's see ... I traveled to three states. I took time out for the flu and a sinus infection. I read a book, tried a few new recipes, attended a concert, and did some serious writing. I visited with friends, attended church, and ate out.

Interesting, isn't it, how quickly a day fills up and then spills over into another day, leaving us exhilarated, exhausted, or perhaps relieved. Before long, the days turn into months and the months into years. After a while we're left scratching our heads, wondering what we did with our time. Some memories of our bygone days have faded or blurred while others are like a hologram card— dimensional and detailed.

Not every day speeds through its allotted hours, of course. How well I remember thinking when I was in labor with each of my sons, "This day will never end!" Then followed the endless stacks of diapers to change and formula to mix, and I wondered if I would get through some of those ammonia-filled days of spit-up. Yet in no time at all I was packing away the baby clothes and unpacking the bank account to assist with their first cars. And when they left home for good, the dirty diapers weren't what remained paramount in my memory; rather, the nursery rhymes, the patty-cakes, and the lullabies were cradled in this mama's heart.

I love that a day has boundaries so I can measure it. From sunrise to sunset, from morning to evening, from a sunlit day to a starlit night, hours collect into a lifetime. As I reflect on my collection, I'm reminded what a gift life is and, therefore, how precious each twenty-four-hour increment is. I also realize that the days I thought would never end are some of the sweeter memories that I hold up now like a multi-faceted diamond refracting light.

One of those sparkling facets is God's extravagant grace, which has been so clearly extended to me throughout my life's journey. He helped me to take the next step on the good days and on the bad—especially the bad.

Dear friend, embrace your day—this day—it is a gift. Take the Lord's hand. He will help you to unwrap the day and then to celebrate it. And his grace will be sufficient for any need you have.

Whatever marches into your day, remember who is the Lion of Judah and the Lamb of God. He tallies our days and tends our nights. He who paid the ultimate price to give us life holds us safely in his eternal hands.

All the days ordained for me were written in your book before one of them came to be.

PSALM 139:16

Imagine That!

Two days ago I was sitting in a hospital lounge waiting for our first grandchild to be born. No, let me restate that. I was *not* sitting; I was pacing. Back and forth, back and forth, attentively listening for a tiny cry or footsteps of someone, anyone, bearing good news. I was both excited and exhausted as the hours ticked by ... five hours, seven hours, nine hours, and then finally, Justin Robert Clairmont was born! He was seven pounds, thirteen ounces, and twenty-two inches long with red hair. Yes-s-s!

After word arrived that all was well, we four grandparents waited with bated breath for our first glimpse of this child who would forever hold our hearts in his hands. That's when I saw a picture that I'll always think of as expressing God's boundless love. The surgery doors swung open (our daughter-in-law had an emergency cesarean), and I saw Jason, my youngest son, walking toward me carrying his firstborn son. My baby was carrying his baby. Wow!

If ever we doubt God's love, we need only observe a baby we deeply care for and then take the feelings of love that bubble up in our hearts and multiply them by infinity. Then we'll have a sense — just a sense, mind you — of God's boundless love.

I find that imagining the vastness of God's love is as close as I can come to measuring it. Perhaps that's why, when the Lord designed us, he included our capacity for imagination. He knew we wouldn't "get it" if we had to weigh his love next to our own puny experiences and abilities to love. He knew we would need to think beyond ourselves and so — *voilà!* — imagination.

Some of my favorite "imagining" verses are found in Job 38 in which the Lord expands Job's mind with thoughts beyond himself. God quizzes Job as to his whereabouts when God created the universe in order to help Job understand the Lord's majestic spaciousness.

"Where were you when I laid the foundation of the earth?" (Job 38:4 NASB).

This absolute statement of proclamation could read, "I laid the foundation of the world before you were a sparkle in your momma's eye!"

Can you visualize laying the earth's foundation? Les and I just purchased a home that is being built, but by the time we made the decision to buy, the foundation already had been poured and the walls were up. Even though I can picture the big excavation trucks digging out the hole, the cement truck pouring the footings and foundation, and the bricklayers building the walls for our home, I can't conceive of how one would go about laying the world's foundation. You would need a cement mixer the size of the Western Hemisphere!

"Where were you [Job] . . . when the morning stars sang together and all the sons of God shouted for joy?" (Job 38:4, 7 NASB).

Can you conceive of the morning stars singing? I love all kinds of music: Celine Dion, Michael Bolton, Andrea Bocelli, Mandy Patinkin, The Martins. . . . Music moves me. I mean, have you heard Mandy Patinkin sing "Over the Rainbow"? Exquisite. I cry almost every time I hear it. Or have you heard Celine Dion and Luciano Pavarotti sing "I Hate You Then I Love You"? Oh, mama mia! And yet I'm certain that, if we teamed up all these gifted singers for one grand performance, they would not, could not, hold a candle to the concert of the morning stars. Of course, I, like Job, wasn't there for the performance, so I'm left imagining.

"Have you [Job] ever in your life commanded the morning, and caused the dawn to know its place?" (Job 38:12 NASB).

I commanded my children when they were young (now they command me), and according to Les, I've commanded him a time or two, but I confess I wouldn't begin to know how to give instruction to the morning or the dawn. At times I've wanted to call off a day, but alas, I didn't have that kind of celestial clout.

Our magnificent God, however, knows the beginning, the end, and beyond. He calls the stars by name, and he has planned and recorded each and every day—including the day my first grandson was born. Imagine that!

Now that, folks, is boundless—boundless love.

The Great Expanse

As a child, I required assistance to grab the monkey bars. (Actually, I still need help to reach them.) An adult would lift me up, while my tummy did flip-flops, until I had a firm grip. Then I was released and had to support my own weight. With hand over fist, hand over fist, I would attempt to make my grueling way from rung to rung across the great expanse. But almost always the pull of my weight would be too much, fear would mount as my fingers slipped, and soon I would topple to the ground.

In the same way, sometimes my grip on God's love slips. That's when I need his help to find my way home, across the great expanse.

God's fearless love not only assists us but also catches us when we fall. Fearless love is sensitive to the truth that we are too little for high things. Fearless love will support us in our efforts to reach beyond ourselves. And fearless love will steady us until we reach the safety of the other side. I like that . . . a lot.

I'm not sure if my humanity or my insecurity is responsible, but I'm given to the misconception that, when I slip and mess up, I must earn my way back into God's good graces. *Surely the process of reconciliation couldn't be as simple as regret and confession,* I tell myself. My sins seem inexcusable, especially considering how long I've known the Lord.

I'm grateful I'm not God. His heart, unlike mine, isn't narrow. Only his path is. And it's a slim strip because he knows we need boundaries to keep us from losing our way.

Aging Miriam, Moses' sister and a leader to the wandering Hebrews, stepped outside the boundaries by usurping God's authority. So she was struck with leprosy and cast out of the camp. There Miriam, the once revered leader, sat with a withered body, calling out, "Unclean, unclean!" when anyone approached her. She had lost her grip; the weightiness of her sin had pulled her down.

The angst of Miriam's heart, the humiliation of her circumstances, must have flooded her with fear. Separated from everything and everyone she loved, Miriam huddled in her personal agony.

My heart aches when I read of Miriam, for I know what it's like to be "unclean" from my sins and to feel like an outcast. I find it frightening to be alone with myself and to face my leprous condition. But I've learned that humiliation often leads to reconciliation, for, as Madeleine L'Engle says, "I know that when I am most monstrous, I am most in need of love." When we get to the end of ourselves, behold: there, at the threshold of change, is God's love that has no fear of the leper in us.

In both Miriam's story and mine we experienced an invitation back into the camp. The Lord longs for our return. Miriam's invitation was sent via the honored prayers of her brothers, Moses and Aaron. To his credit, Moses, who could have been offended, prayed for his offender. We should be so big.

The Scriptures act as a map to help us journey across the great expanse from enemy territory to the safety of the Promised Land. Along the way, we observe the Israelites, who lost their grip and regained it, and we find hope and insight. And while Scripture serves as a life-map for us, God's fearless love acts as a safety net to catch us and then to infuse us with the courage to try again and again and again ... until we finally reach the other side. Whew!

I don't know what the future may hold, but I know who holds the future.

ROBERT ABERNATHY

Take Me Out to the Ball Game

When I was a youngster, I loved Saturday mornings. I would rise early without parental prompting, slide into my jeans and sweatshirt, gobble down a bowl of Snap, Crackle, and Pop dappled with sliced bananas, and head out the door to join my neighborhood friends. Almost always the boys, who happened to form the majority on the block, would decide to play baseball.

I loved competitive sports, except for one aspect—the process of choosing up sides. Being in the minority, I always was the choosee rather than the chooser. And no self-respecting boy would pick a girl until all the boys were divvied out. That was an unwritten code.

I found these intentional slights at best degrading and at worst humiliating. No, I wasn't a great player, but I was, as my kinfolk would say, dad-burn better than some of the fellows who were picked afore me.

Intentional is not "Oops, I didn't mean to do that" but "Here, take that." It's a deliberate decision. And nothing is more demeaning than to know you weren't considered up to par, you couldn't make the cut, and you were a deliberate reject.

On the other hand (I'm grateful there is another hand), when I hit high school and played in girls' organized sports, I frequently was chosen—and may I point out intentionally—usually among the first. *Y-e-s!* There is nothing like knowing you are preferred, esteemed, appreciated, applauded, and sought after. Although, sometimes we might wish to remain anonymous—like when the softball game turns to hardball. . .

Gideon was a man filled with fears and unanswered questions when suddenly, in the midst of his hardships, an angel of the Lord asked him to step up to the plate. Certain there had been a mistake, Gideon began to explain to the angel his error.

You see, Israel had been disobedient to the Lord so God had allowed the Midianites to shut out his people. The land was stripped of its crops and animals, and the Israelites, who had taken to the hills, resorted to hiding in caves. More enemies were swarming the land than fans attending the World Series.

And now this angel was asking Gideon to be the captain of God's team and to lead his people into the championship circle. Gideon tried to negotiate with the messenger by highlighting his own deficiencies. First he confessed to the heavenly scout his weak heritage, and then Gideon admitted he was the youngest in his family—why, he was just a kid!

When those tactics failed to dissuade the recruiter, Gideon asked for a divine sign (as if a visit from an angel wasn't a billboard statement). The Lord graciously accommodated Captain Gideon's faltering faith; yet even after the Lord gave Gideon a clear sign, he requested a repeat performance. I mean, this guy just couldn't believe the Lord had *intentionally* selected him.

As I read Gideon's story, I want to yell, "Excuse me, Gid, but the Lord chooses you on purpose! He knows your family history, your age, even your reluctance, and he still prefers you to all others. So what's your problem?"

Actually, even as I ask that of Gideon, the impact of it hits home with me. Truth be known, I too have those times in my life when I can't believe the Lord would choose *me*. Why, I can name off a teamload of others who are far better qualified, who have more impressive credentials, and who haven't struck out in their lives as consistently as I have. And yet he chooses me. How humbling for me. How gracious of him.

To know that God has a plan and we fit into it is proof enough to me of his intentional love.

Lord, thank you that you don't keep track of our strikeouts or even our homeruns. Instead, you simply and graciously ask us to step up to the plate. To be on your team. Wow!

Much Ado About Much

My husband, Les, is a lavish kind of guy. If a little works, then he'll do a lot. And if a lot is necessary to fill the bill, then he'll double that. His "giver" is stuck on muchness. Lucky me!

Actually, I've spent a good deal of time trying to temper his extravagant heart—although, just between you and me, I hope I never succeed. I mean, who buys a Ferrari and then has a governor installed? (For those of you who are auto-challenged, a governor is one of those deals they put on cars to keep them from going too fast.) Instead, one looks forward to opening that baby's throttle all the way!

I must say, I find it delightful to unwrap a gift from a lavish giver, to find something inside that takes my breath away. I've also discovered that taking someone who is prone to lavishness with you when you shop for clothes is a good strategy. That way, when you turn boringly practical and decide to settle for less than the best, Mr. Lavish steps in to rescue you. Saleswomen constantly ask me where I found Les since he's always prodding, "Are you only going to buy one outfit? Oh, honey, please get them both."

When our two sons were young, every year at Easter I would send Les scurrying to buy baskets for them. I would carefully instruct him to buy small ones because the kids didn't need a lot of junk food to carve craters in their bicuspids. But every year Mr. Extravagant would come home with some outrageous offering: stuffed rabbits the size of blimps, wagons — yes, wagons — full of candy, grocery sacks bulging with jelly beans, soap bubbles by the jug . . .

I remember one time Les found an unusual teapot he thought I'd enjoy adding to my collection. Then, he decided, if one was great, two would be stupendous. So he bought identical teapots. I thought I was seeing double. This man just doesn't understand moderation.

Moderate means "reasonable, measured, and restrained." It's a wondrous concept, if one is trying to cut costs or lose weight. Yet, even though the principle of moderation fits us like a glove when we speak of food consumption, notice how our interest dwindles when we speak of, say, sky illumination. I mean, imagine if the Lord had been moderate with the stars that he pressed into the velvet night. What if he had tossed out only a handful? Why, we would miss out on the breathtaking moments when we gaze heavenward — not to mention the light source.

Or what if the Lord had become tightfisted when he chiseled the mountains with artistic brilliance? Why, we would have no Grand Canyon, no Swiss Alps, and the Himalayas would be a heap of dust blowing about in the wind.

And what if our only water source was the oceans, but no lakes, streams, or brooks existed? Why, where would we snag a bass, run a stringer of bluegills, or go fly-fishing? And think of all the barefoot little boys and girls who would miss out on catching pollywogs, turtles, frogs, and snakes. And where would those scalawag fellows take flying, body-smacking leaps into cool ponds on scorching days? Or float their latest hand-carved sailboats?

Here's the best news yet: God wasn't moderate in his love but *lavished* it on us at Calvary. Christ became heaven's door that we might enter in. And we don't have to wait until death to experience heaven's boundless, exquisite love. Christ rescues us daily in myriad ways from settling for less than his dazzling best.

A hymn writer penned it this way: "Heaven came down and glory filled my soul." The risen Christ in us now and through eternity—how lavish can you get?

> *May showers of blessing*
> *fall lavishly on you today*
> *and fill your soul with glory!*

Jesus' conspicuously unconventional behavior caused others to take a second gander. I mean, this humble man made divine proclamations that caused even the clergy to huddle. Dismayed by Jesus' bizarre ways and his influence on the populace, the religious leaders plotted his demise.

What is it about "different" that threatens us so? We seem to have a need for things to be as we've always known them to feel safe—even if the way they've been ain't all that spiffy. And heaven forbid if anyone thinks *us* odd.

I've noted those hesitant qualities in myself at times. The unknown, the peculiar, and the strange are off-putting.

Folks were abuzz when the off-putting Bethlehem man showed up in their town and healed the afflicted on the Sabbath. Jesus left people aghast and in awe as he created outlandish controversy wherever he went. He deliberately stepped across traditional lines, and he did so in such miraculous and peculiar ways: turning water into wine, touching lepers, forgiving prostitutes, raising the dead, keeping company with social outcasts, and casting out demons—to name just a few of his startling choices.

Jesus had a *way,* and it certainly wasn't the people's way or, come to think of it, our way either.

Thank heavens Christ came to rescue us from our smallness, our emptiness, our busyness, our loneliness, and our sinfulness. Left on my own, without the Lord's intervention, I squander precious time, I hold onto grudges as if they were my best friends, I pass judgments as generously as police officers hand out tickets, and I plump up my weaknesses like a down pillow.

I'm grateful Christ hasn't left us to flail about in our inadequacies, but instead he guides us toward transformation. Just listen to some of the unnatural changes that are necessary if we are to be like him.

"Love your enemies" (Luke 6:27).

Hello? I don't do that great of a job loving those I truly care about, so what are the chances I'm going to embrace some bozo who gets on my last nerve? I'll tell you: absolutely zero without Christ.

"Pray for those who persecute you" (Matt. 5:44).

Last week some lady took the parking spot I was waiting for, and I wanted to deck her. (I'm not boasting; I'm confessing.) Imagine if she had committed some *really* annoying act! Why, I'd probably be doing community service for the next few years.

"Do not store up for yourselves treasures on earth" (Matt. 6:19).

Uh-oh. Does that include my teapot collection? Or my grandmother's ring? Surely that doesn't mean my collection of children's books? Or my antique desk?

Those are just a few of the character issues Christ wants to address in us. He longs for us to experience radical transformation of what comes naturally. Isn't that outlandish? All I can say is it's a good thing our God is big because, if we're going to be that different from our human nature, he's going to be very busy. Talk about a full-time job!

Do you think the Lord's ways seem outlandish to us because just capturing a glimpse of him causes us to gasp with wonder? Because he's so much more than we can think or imagine?

Perhaps that's how Isaiah felt when he saw the Lord sitting on a throne, high and lofty. Listen in to Isaiah's response: "Woe to me! . . . I am ruined! For I am a man of unclean lips, and I live among a people of unclean lips, and my eyes have seen the King, the LORD Almighty" (Isa. 6:5). Seeing the Lord caused Isaiah to realize his own unfit condition, for it stood in direct contrast to the Lord of hosts' holiness.

Yes, the Lord makes seemingly outrageous requests of us. But when we see him as he is, we long to be different, truly transformed—even outlandish, like him.

Now therefore, if ye will obey my voice indeed, and keep my covenant, then ye shall be a peculiar treasure unto me.

EXODUS 19:5 KJV

Moving On

Okay, here's a grandma story ... I can't help myself. I'm so smitten with this darling boy. I knew it would be cool to be a grandparent, but I didn't realize how deep and significant it would feel.

So here's the story: When my daughter-in-law, Danya, was taken into surgery for a C-section, our little one stunned the doctor with his outlandish birth. When the incision was made, Justin slipped out his hand as if to greet the world, but when the doctor reached for it, Justin pulled his hand back inside his mommy's tummy and headed north. By the time the doctor finally caught him, she had to bring Justin into this world bottom side up, which she said was a first for her—a breech C-section!

Now, my take on this is that Justin was comfortable and felt safe right where he was. He appreciated being tucked close to his mom's heart and had no desire to have things change.

I know how that feels, and I bet you do too. Just when you have all your pillows fluffed and you have cozied in under the comforter, the doorbell buzzes, the telephone jingles, or the smoke detector squeals.

Recently I realized that I was going to add to my long saga of wandering (moving repeatedly). The home we live in now is unsuitable for my husband's growing disabilities, which is a legitimate need; but I confess I'm finding it difficult to change addresses again. I have loved this home, with all its nooks and crannies and lovely walking gardens. The cove ceilings and wide woodwork suit my love of antiques and my appreciation of history, and the small rooms have lent themselves to my enjoyment of cozy spaces. The location too has been a pleasure. Within minutes we can walk to town or stroll to the farmer's market on the weekends.

Yet I want, of course, what is best for Les. And I know that a year from now, I will take delight in our new home's special features: open floor plan, generous kitchen, and lovely view. For now, though, I'm wanting, like Justin, to scramble into the nearest hiding place and take refuge. But then I think about Justin's outrageous birth and, well, I just don't think I'd do "breech" well. I'm too old, and all that blood rushing to my head would leave me dizzier than I already am.

I wonder — it dizzies me to even imagine — how Christ brought himself to leave the security and purity of heaven to join us here on this sin-polluted planet. Talk about an outlandish birth! God himself born from a woman in a dirty barn. I wonder if Jesus was inclined to skedaddle back into the safety of his mom's womb when the time came for him to become God incarnate.

And talk about giving up an ideal location before he was conceived. . . . From what I've heard, it doesn't get any better than Glory. The views in heaven . . . well, we can only imagine. I have yet to see a street of gold, a rainbow of emerald, a wall of jasper, or a pearl gate. And can you conjure up in your mind what heavenly music might sound like? I try, but I know my efforts fall short. The best I can do is Handel's *Messiah* on surround sound.

In Philippians 2 a melody rings for our souls. Listen in:

Your attitude should be the same as that of Christ Jesus: Who, being in very nature God, did not consider equality with God something to be grasped, but made himself nothing, taking the very nature of a servant. . . . He humbled himself and became obedient to death—even death on a cross! (vv. 5–8)

Because of what Christ did willingly for us, we then can and should walk, skip, and run willingly toward embracing his servant attitude. That thought causes me to ask myself, "What's giving up a house on this sod anyway?" One day I'll have a mansion. Hallelujah!

I've decided little Justin reached out his hand to test the weather. Dear grandson, fear not! There is One who will starlight your darkest night and see you through till Glory.

"We got a home in Gloryland that outshines the sun."
Now, that's a move I'm looking forward to!

Pin the Tale on the Donkey

I know I'm dating myself when I admit that, growing up, I loved to watch Francis the talking mule movies on television. Now, for those youngsters who haven't a clue who Francis is, he was a real mule who starred in several movies. He managed to get into and out of a lot of predicaments but talked only to his master.

Those of you who were Francis fans know the old chap was quite the character and often lived up to his species' reputation of being downright ornery, especially when it worked to his advantage. Francis would at times plop down and refuse to budge, regardless how much others would pull, tug, bribe, or plead.

Which reminds me of another story . . . but this one is a donkey tale, a true saga about a female animal with the gift of gab. What a surprise.

Balaam, an Old Testament prophet, was being enticed by financial gain to call down a curse on the Israelites, God's beloved people. God had a message for Balaam but apparently was having a little problem getting Balaam's attention.

Then one day Balaam mounted his donkey and headed for the plains of Moab when, along the way, the angel of the Lord stood in the path with his sword drawn. The donkey saw the angel and turned off the road, trotting into a field. Balaam, oblivious to the angel's presence, struck the donkey to force her back on the road.

The rider and beast continued their trip when, lo and behold, the angel appeared again. Only this time he stood on a tapered path with walls on both sides. To avoid the angel, the donkey had to press against the wall, scraping Balaam's leg on the rock. Balaam throttled her for this unseemly behavior.

A third time the heavenly visitor blocked a narrow path, which left the donkey no space to pass. So she lay down in the road. Balaam was livid! He took a stick to his stubborn donkey.

Then the most amazing thing happened: the animal spoke. "Hey, you bozo, stop flapping that stick. You know it's not my way to be obstinate. I've carried your carcass faithfully for years, so get off my back." (Okay, so this is my version. Read the real conversation for yourself in Numbers 22.)

Balaam answered the donkey, "You made me look bad in front of my friends. You're lucky I didn't have a sword, or I'd have had donkey burgers for lunch!" (Yes, my version.)

Then the Lord opened Balaam's eyes, and he saw the angel with sword in hand. Balaam bowed down. (Funny how fast we change our stance when the sword is in another's hand.) The angel then informed Balaam that, *thanks to his donkey,* the angel didn't have to kill Balaam.

Wow! Who was the stubborn one? Not the faithful donkey, but the faulty prophet. Balaam had insisted on heading in the wrong direction for the wrong reasons, and a lowly donkey did her best to spare his life. What a picture — a pompous prophet and a divine donkey.

But another picture comes into focus as well. This one is worthy of being enlarged and framed. It's the picture of God's stubborn love for this misguided man. Look at the mercy God showed Balaam over and over again. Why, that angel could have lopped off old Balaam's head with one flick of the sword. He could have skewered Balaam when he was pressed against the wall or parted Balaam's hair clear to his navel when the donkey lay down. But instead God allowed the little servant animal to spare Balaam's life.

While *stubborn* often denotes rebellious resistance like Balaam's insistence to head in the wrong (heart) direction, *stubborn* also exemplifies God's unswerving devotion to his people to help them find their way.

Can you find yourself in this story? Are you Balaam, determined to do your own thing regarding your life direction? Or are you a servant at heart, the kind God allows to see what others miss?

Perhaps, to be on the safe side, you might want to pray this prayer with me:

Lord, if I'm on the wrong road, open my eyes that I might see the truth. May I be wise enough to learn from your servants along the way. And thank you, merciful Father, for your stubborn love. Amen.

Unstrung

After my mother-in-law Lena's death, I was given several of her necklaces, including a long strand of pearls. The first time I wore them was on a speaking trip, and as I rushed down the hotel's hall to catch the airport shuttle, the strand broke. I stood helplessly as the pearls bounced away in all directions.

I called to the bellhop, who was twenty steps ahead of me, to wait while I tried to collect them. I had hoped he would help me, but I guess it wasn't in his job description. The pearls weren't expensive, but they were priceless to me because they had belonged to someone I loved. I carefully gathered as many as I could and carried them home in my purse with hopes I could have them restrung.

At one point in my life, I, like Lena's necklace, had frayed until finally my life fell apart. My emotions, like skittish pearls, ricocheted off walls, which left me unstrung. I didn't understand why I was so emotionally frail and fearful or why those around me weren't able to help me gather up my broken parts and put me back together.

But guess what I learned. It wasn't in their job description. It wasn't that they wouldn't; it was that they couldn't. Jesus is the only true Redeemer. He is the only one who can restring my life and yours, who can retrieve all that we've lost, and who can give us back our value.

In the New Testament we have the joy of listening in as the seeking, the lost, the broken, the forgotten, the paralyzed, and the skeptical gather around Jesus. The Lord, who understood their frayed and scattered condition, prescribed truth, direction, wholeness, mercy, forgiveness, love, and liberty for all who came with an ear to hear and a heart to receive.

Interestingly, the ones who were the most receptive were the most obviously damaged (lepers, crippled, grief stricken, neglected). That confirms what I've always suspected: The things we fear (pain, failure, disgrace, rejection, limitations) are ultimately some of our finest teachers, educating us in compassion, grace, wisdom, and understanding.

I have great empathy for those who struggle with erratic emotions because I know how overwhelming unpredictable feelings can be, feelings that flood in with such force they affect even your physical well-being. In my emotionally chaotic years, I had more symptoms than a dog has fleas. But you can treat fleas, whereas neurotic symptoms only leave the doctor scratching his head and the patient feeling hopeless. My fear-based illnesses kept me living a restricted, suffocating lifestyle.

At first, in my agoraphobic years, I coddled my fearful feelings to protect myself. Instead, my indulgence magnified the problem until one day I realized that I had only a few pearls left on my necklace, and I was about to lose those. I was already in a relationship with Christ, but if I was to survive, I would have to trust him at new levels. I would have to face my fears.

Slowly, as I inched toward freedom, Christ assisted me in finding my lost and hidden emotions. Pearl by priceless pearl, he restrung my necklace. He taught me to trade in my panic for the pearl of his peace, to switch my weakness for the pearl of his strength, and to exchange my fear for the pearl of his fearlessness.

I love the chorus, "Turn your eyes upon Jesus, look full in his wonderful face, and the things of earth will grow strangely dim in the light of his glory and grace." And that, my friend, includes our fears. They will wither in his presence while we grow in grace.

During my healing trek, I learned I was priceless to him because of his boundless love for me. And that's how he feels about you! So, no matter how unstrung you feel, or how many pearls you've lost, he longs to gather you up in his arms and calm your every fear.

Errors, like straws,
upon the surface flow;
he who would search for
pearls must dive below.

JOHN DRYDEN

You've Got Mail

When I was a child, I loved to watch my mamaw (grandmother) pull out bundles of letters tied together with yarn from her trunk that sat at the end of her bed. Also inside the trunk were photographs, crocheted potholders she gave as gifts, assorted small treasures, and handmade quilts used to warm up winter. But she valued the letters most, for these were words from those whom she loved. And she carefully read and reread them until they were imprinted on her heart.

Letters bring people near — even if they are on the other side of the world, in the midst of a war, or long past the edges of this finite earth. I've been reading Winston and Clementine Churchill's letters, including wartime notes, which they wrote to each other over a period of fifty-six years. Their correspondence was full of tension and tenderness as they shared their greatest fears and their deepest love. I was impressed with the frequency of their exchanges, many times daily.

Winston and Clementine obviously were devoted to each other, yet the letters also contain some heated moments. Whew, what a relief! When others share their human frailty we're encouraged that we're not the only ones who struggle in relationships.

The record of the Churchills' struggles left clear imprints in their correspondence because the couple wrote letters to each other even when they were sitting in the same room. Clementine realized early on in their relationship that her reactive personality and her tendency to exaggerate to make a point with Winston caused unnecessary strain between them. So, to keep the home atmosphere more cordial and loving and also out of a need to be heard, Clementine would write to Winston about potentially volatile issues, thereby avoiding temperament conflicts. She found that, as she wrote a letter, she remained more objective and less vehement. Therefore, Winston, instead of tuning out his wife, would carefully consider her input. So was born what their daughter called "the house post advocacy," which would not only assist this notable couple in a personal way but would also allow the rest of the world to one day listen in. And so we gain insights into the couple and how they turned communication challenges into memorable communiqués.

Speaking of listening in, I have greatly benefited from the apostle Paul's letters. For instance, when he penned a letter to the new Christians at Philippi, he wrote not from a Hilton suite but from a prison — a dark, dank prison. Not exactly an ideal spot for writing inspirational material, yet he did. In fact, he wrote a joyful message that continues to help millions see what it means to rejoice in all situations. I find it's one thing to tell a person what she *should* do, but quite another to share from what you've *experienced* in your own life. Paul's life was filled with hardships, yet in those difficult places he lived out his faith. And it was during those times that he wrote the rich, directional, foundational letters in what eventually became the New Testament.

As I write to you, there sits on my nightstand a bundle of letters, which includes Paul's, held together by a leather cover. They are love letters written to anyone who has a heart to hear of God's boundless, fearless, stubborn, lavish, outlandish, intentional love. These personal letters have been handed down through the ages, that we might know we aren't alone — not alone in our struggles, not alone in our lives. And the truths in these letters, when written on our hearts, make an eternal difference.

I appreciate that the Scriptures are so full of human frailty while also giving us magnificent glimpses of divinity. That leaves us with hope. Imagine if we allowed the Bible to become our "house post advocacy," that we might read and reread of the Lord's tender feelings for us, that we might allow his words to be imprinted within us, that we might know his boundless love. Surely our own hearts would overflow in response to his.

Grace to all who love our Lord Jesus Christ with an undying love.

PAUL, IN HIS LETTER TO THE EPHESIANS (6:24)

FAITH

Women of Faith partners with various Christian organizations, including Zondervan, Campus Crusade for Christ International, Crossings Book Club, Integrity Music, International Bible Society, Partnerships, Inc., and World Vision to provide spiritual resources for women.

For more information about Women of Faith or to register for one of our nationwide conferences, call 1-800-49-FAITH.

www.women-of-faith.com

Women of Faith Devotionals

Joy Breaks
Hardcover 0-310-21345-2

We Brake for Joy!
Hardcover 0-310-22042-4
Audio Pages® Abridged Cassettes 0-310-22434-9

OverJoyed!
Hardcover 0-310-22653-8
Audio Pages® Abridged Cassettes
0-310-22760-7

Extravagant Grace
Hardcover 0-310-23125-6
Audio Pages℠ Abridged
Cassettes 0-310-23126-4

Resources for Women of Faith℠

BOOKS/AUDIO

The Joyful Journey	Hardcover	0-310-21344-4
	Softcover	0-310-22155-2
	Audio Pages® Abridged Cassettes	0-310-21454-8
	Daybreak	0-310-97282-5
Bring Back the Joy	Hardcover	0-310-22023-8
	Softcover	0-310-22915-4
	Audio Pages® Abridged Cassettes	0-310-22222-2
Outrageous Joy	Hardcover	0-310-22648-1
	Audio Pages® Abridged Cassettes	0-310-22660-0

WOMEN OF FAITH BIBLE STUDY SERIES

Celebrating Friendship	0-310-21338-X
Discovering Your Spiritual Gifts	0-310-21340-1
Embracing Forgiveness	0-310-21341-X
Experiencing God's Presence	0-310-21343-6
Finding Joy	0-310-21336-3
Growing in Prayer	0-310-21335-5
Knowing God's Will	0-310-21339-8
Strengthening Your Faith	0-310-21337-1

WOMEN OF FAITH WOMEN OF THE BIBLE STUDY SERIES

Deborah: Daring to Be Different for God	0-310-22662-7
Esther: Becoming a Woman God Can Use	0-310-22663-5
Hannah: Entrusting Your Dreams to God	0-310-22667-8
Mary: Choosing the Joy of Obedience	0-310-22664-3
Ruth: Trusting That God Will Provide for You	0-310-22665-1
Sarah: Facing Life's Uncertainties with a Faithful God	0-310-22666-X

WOMEN OF FAITH Zondervan*Groupware*™

Capture the Joy	Video Curriculum Kit	0-310-23096-9
	Leader's Guide	0-310-23101-9
	Participant's Guide	0-310-23099-3

*Inspirio's innovative and elegant gift books
capture the joy and encouragement that is an integral part
of the Women of Faith^{SM} movement.*

Joy for a Woman's Soul
Promises to Refresh Your Spirit
ISBN: 0-310-97717-7

Grace for a Woman's Soul
Reflections to Renew Your Spirit
ISBN: 0-310-97996-X

Simple Gifts
*Unwrapping the Special
Moments of Everyday Life*
ISBN: 0-310-97811-4

Hope for a Woman's Soul
*Meditations to
Energize Your
Spirit*
ISBN: 0-310-98010-0

Padded Hardcover
4 x 7
208 pages

---

*Verses from the New International Version of
the Bible have been collected into these topically arranged volumes
to inspire Women of Faith^{SM} on their spiritual journey.*

Prayers for a Woman of Faith^{SM}
ISBN: 0-310-97336-8

Words of Wisdom
for a Woman of Faith^{SM}
ISBN: 0-310-97390-2

Promises of Joy
for a Woman of Faith^{SM}
ISBN: 0-310-97389-9

Words of Wisdom
for a Woman of Faith^{SM}
ISBN: 0-310-97735-5

Hardcover
5-1/4 X 5-1/4
128 pages

Psalms and Proverbs
for a Woman of Faith^{SM}
ISBN: 0-310-98092-5

Promises of Love
for a Woman of Faith^{SM}
ISBN: 0-310-98249-9

We want to hear from you. Please send your comments about this book to us in care of the address below. Thank you.

ZONDERVAN™

GRAND RAPIDS, MICHIGAN 49530

www.zondervan.com